Learn to Draw!

Learn to draw the easy way using the grid method. With the grid method, a picture is laid out in a square grid. Then the picture is copied to a new grid of equal ratio. Draw the picture, focusing on one grid at a time until the picture is complete.

Learning to draw using grids helps to train your visual memory and observation skills. It allows your eyes and brain to concentrate on just one area to be able to draw it accurately. It can also be used to scale up or down a picture. It has been used for centuries to help artists perfect their skills and practice drawing what is seen.

Once you've mastered the grid method using the practice pictures in this book, you'll be able to use this method to draw any picture you choose.

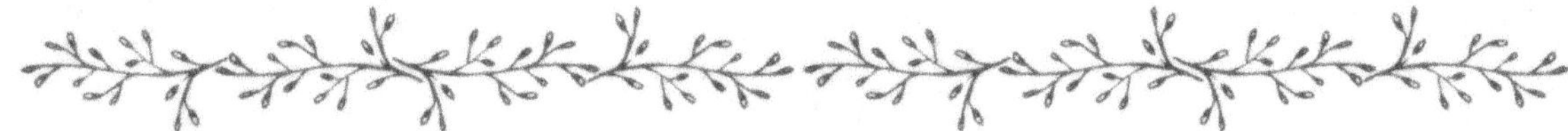

Tips to Get Started

- Focus on one box a time.
- If you get confused, try covering portions of the grid so you can only see small sections at a time.
- Use a pencil and draw lightly at first so you can erase mistakes easily.
- When you're finished, color it to bring your drawing to life.
- Remember to have fun!

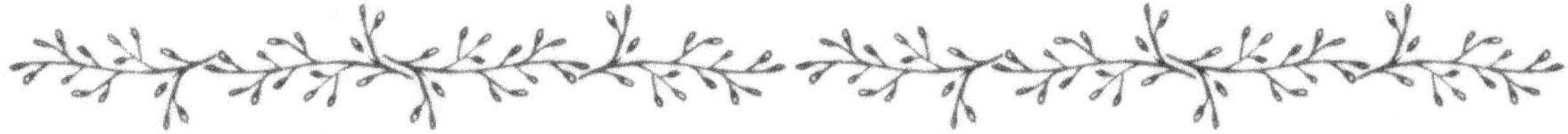

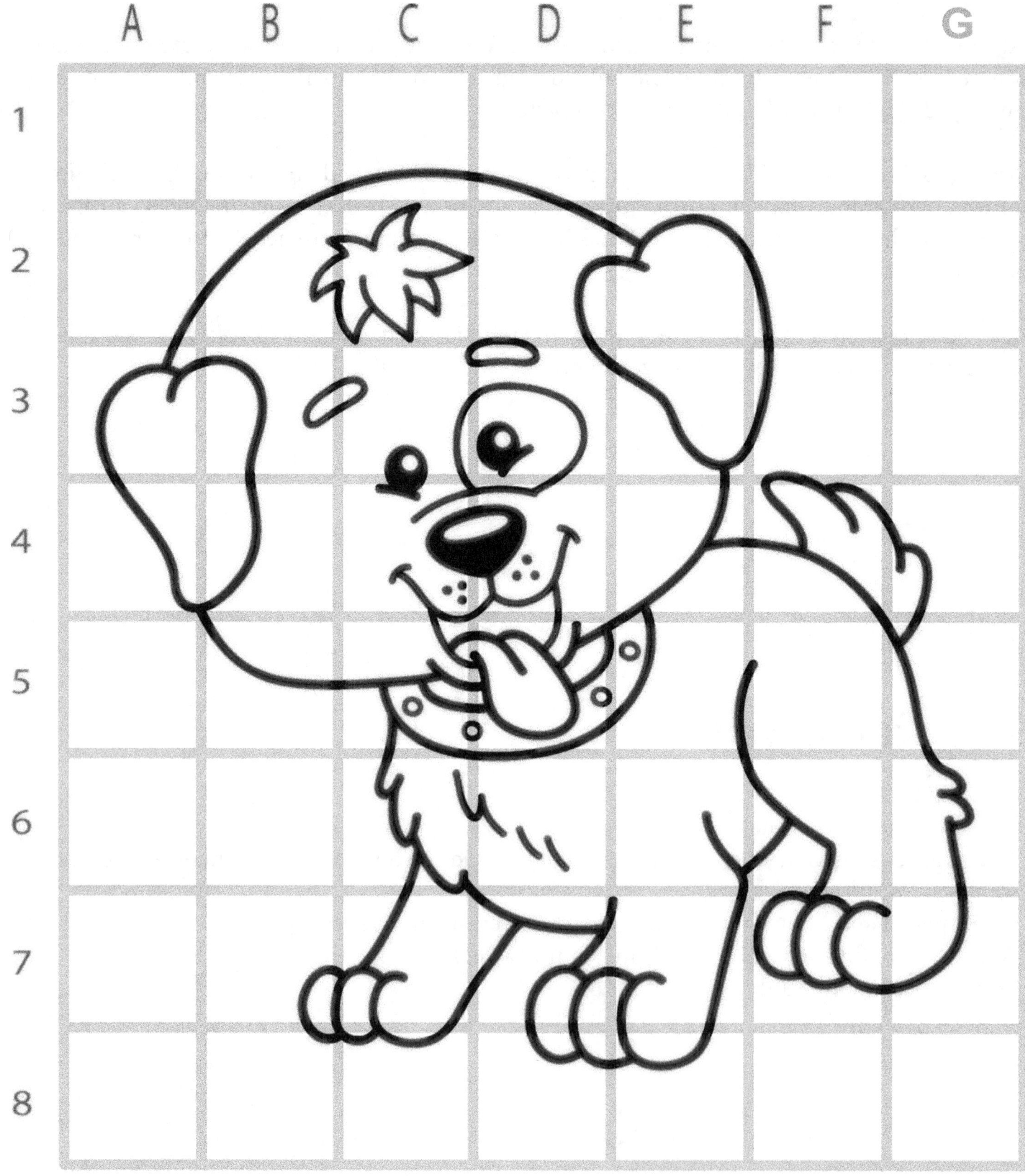

A B C D E F G
1
2
3
4
5
6
7
8

Learn to Draw
Animals
for Kids

Fun Activities for Drawing Using Grids

	A	B	C	D	E	F	G
1							
2							
3							
4							
5							
6							
7							
8							

A B C D E F G
1 2 3 4 5 6 7 8

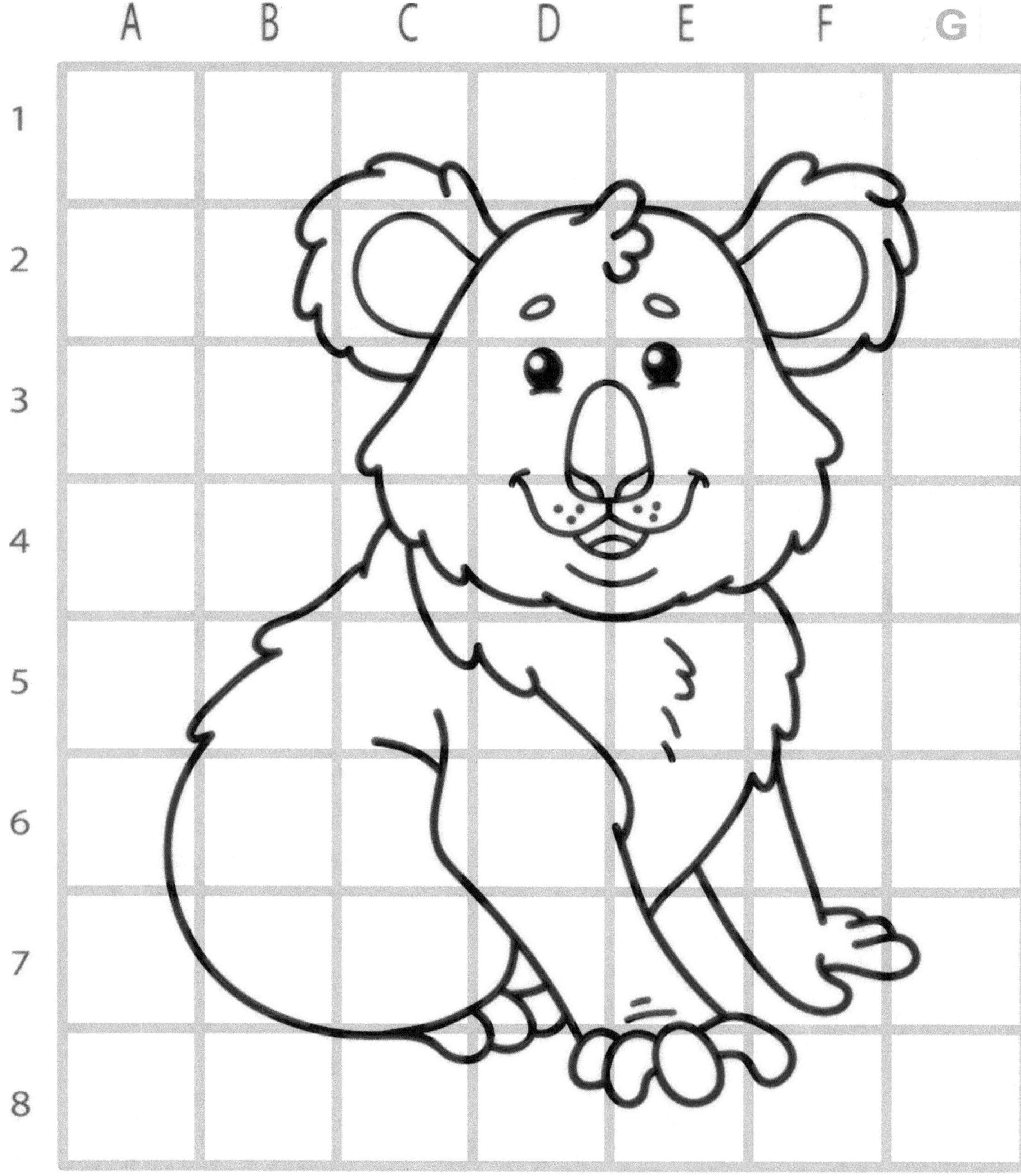

	A	B	C	D	E	F	G
1							
2							
3							
4							
5							
6							
7							
8							

A B C D E F G
1
2
3
4
5
6
7
8

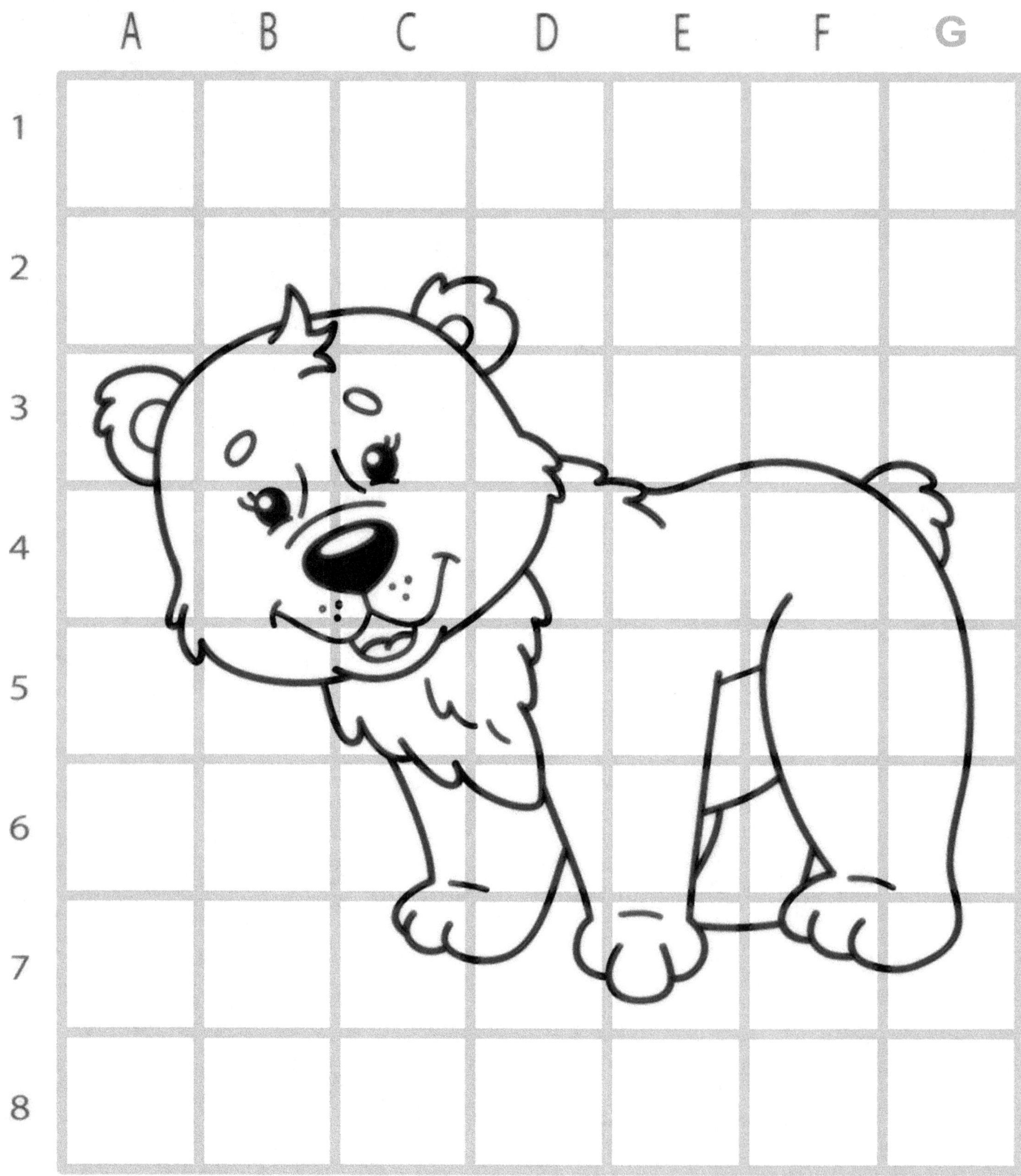

	A	B	C	D	E	F	G
1							
2							
3							
4							
5							
6							
7							
8							

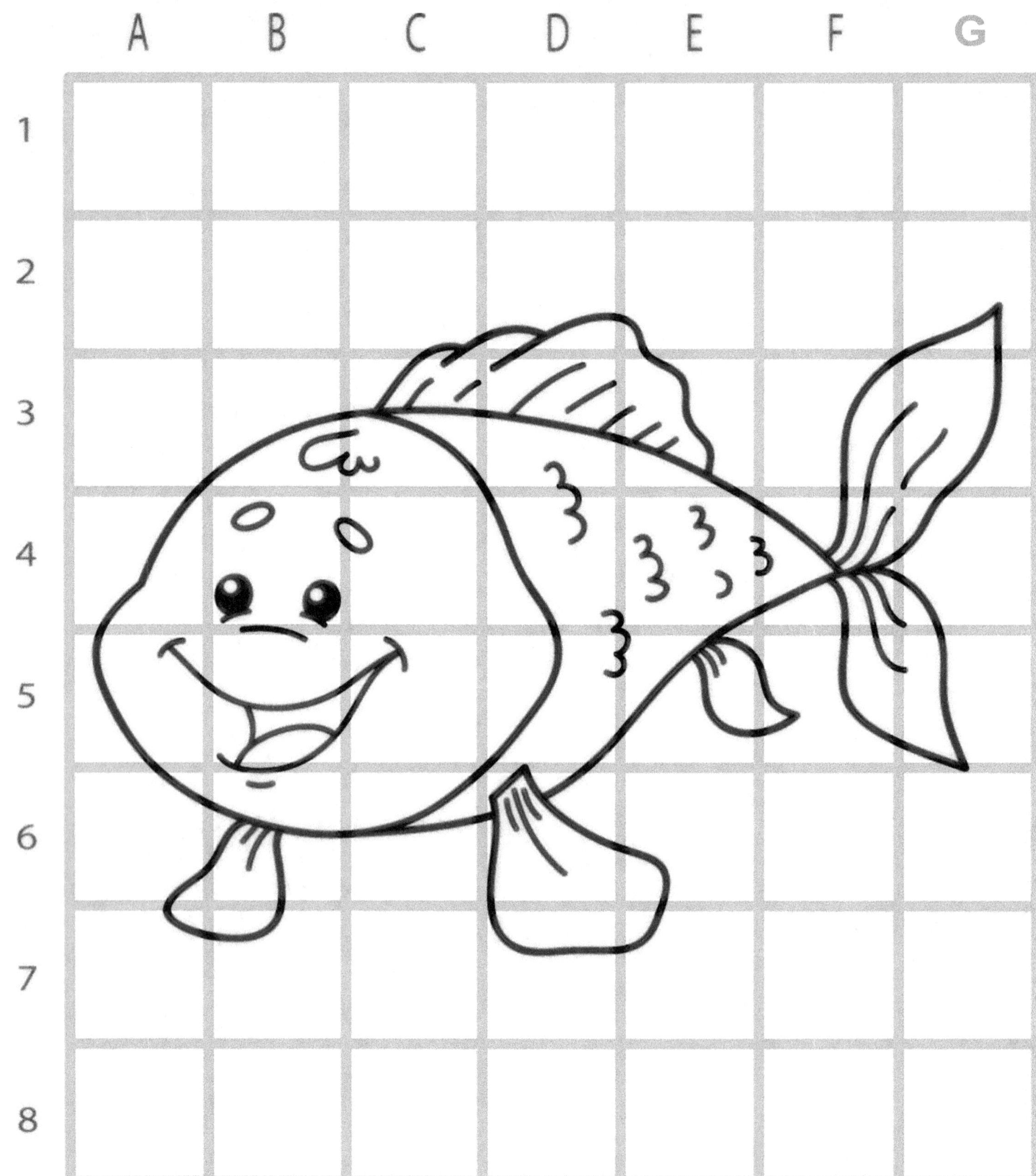

A   B   C   D   E   F   G
1
2
3
4
5
6
7
8

	A	B	C	D	E	F	G
1							
2							
3							
4							
5							
6							
7							
8							

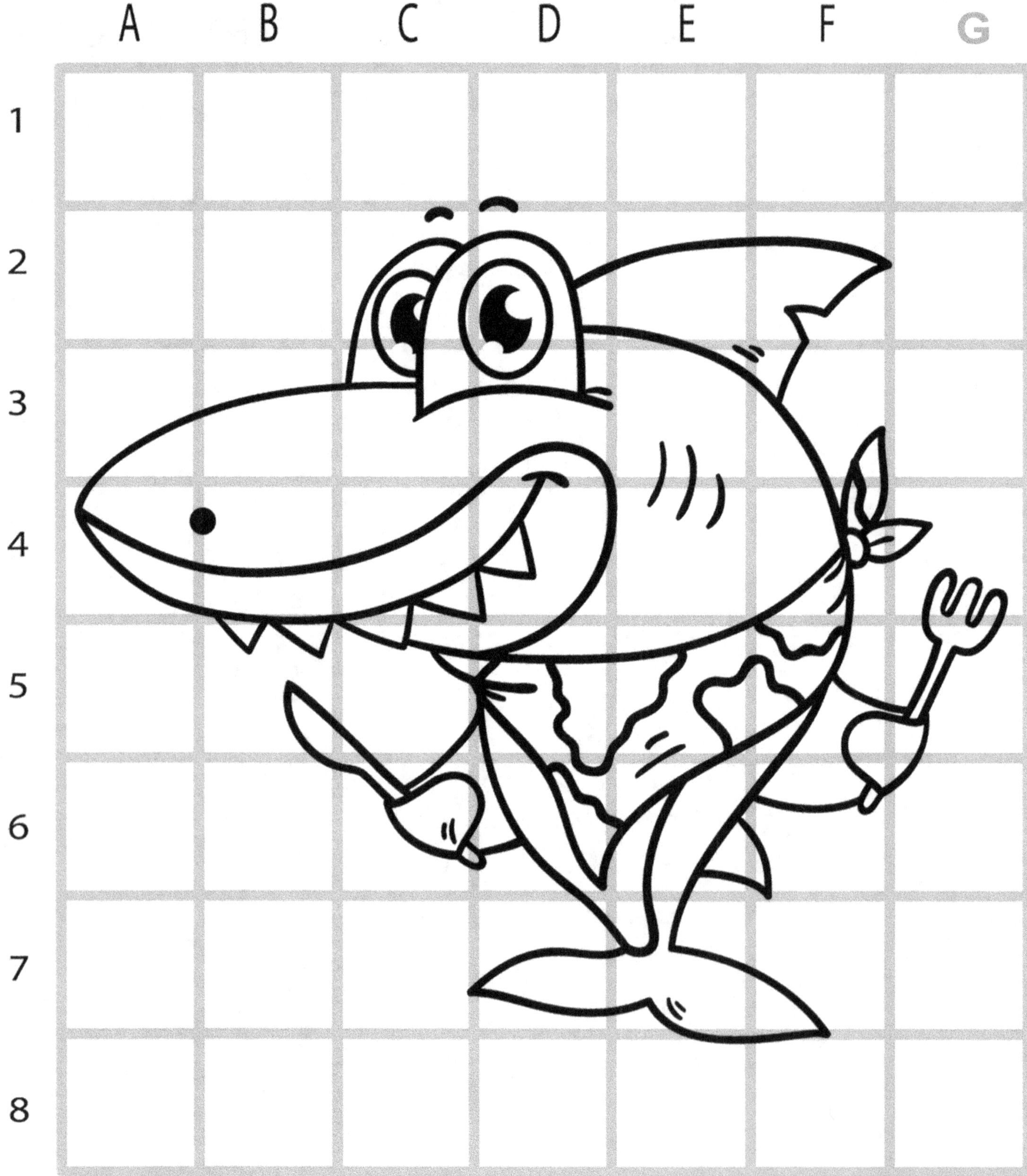

A B C D E F G
1
2
3
4
5
6
7
8

	A	B	C	D	E	F	G
1							
2							
3							
4							
5							
6							
7							
8							

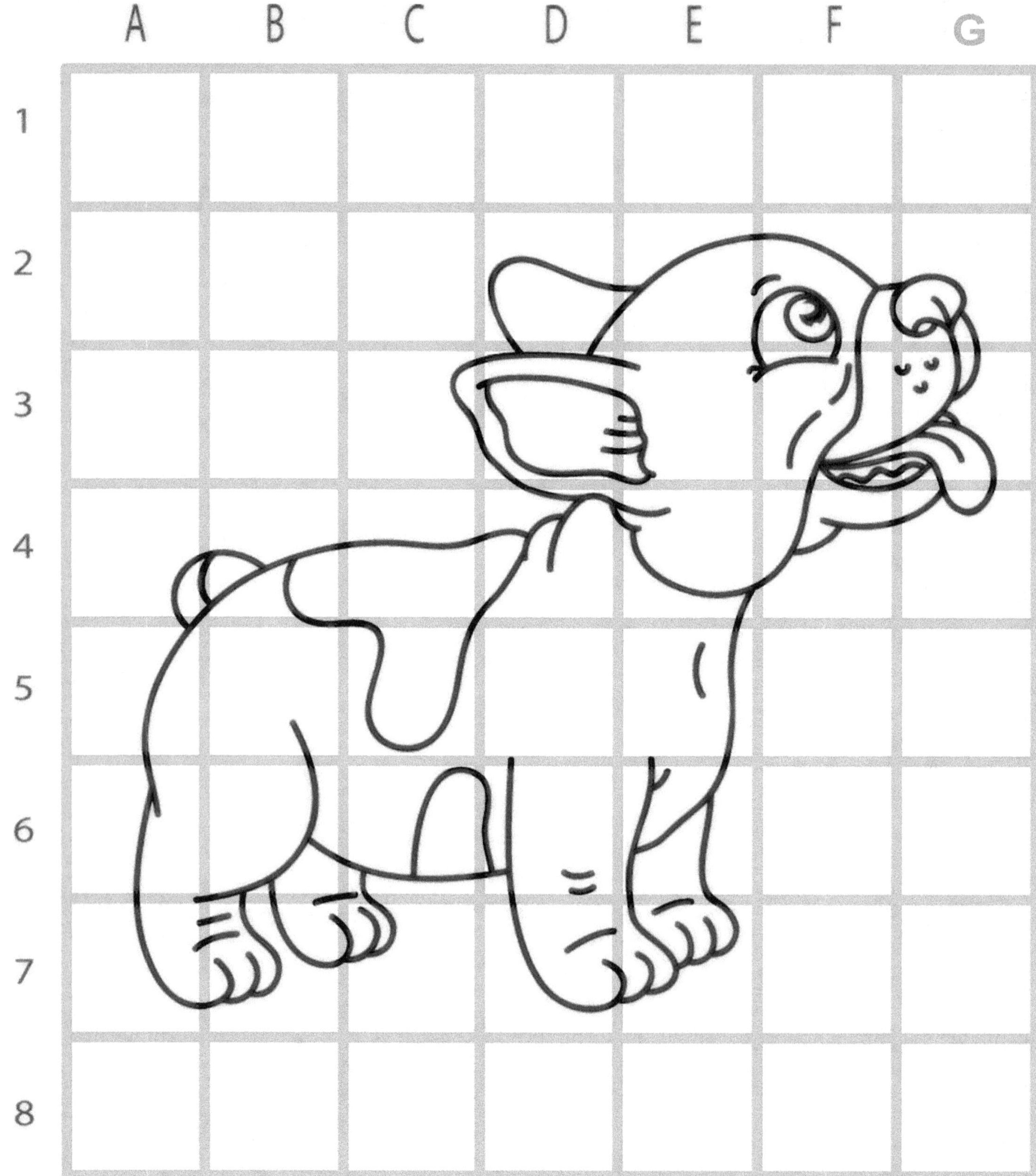

	A	B	C	D	E	F	G
1							
2							
3							
4							
5							
6							
7							
8							

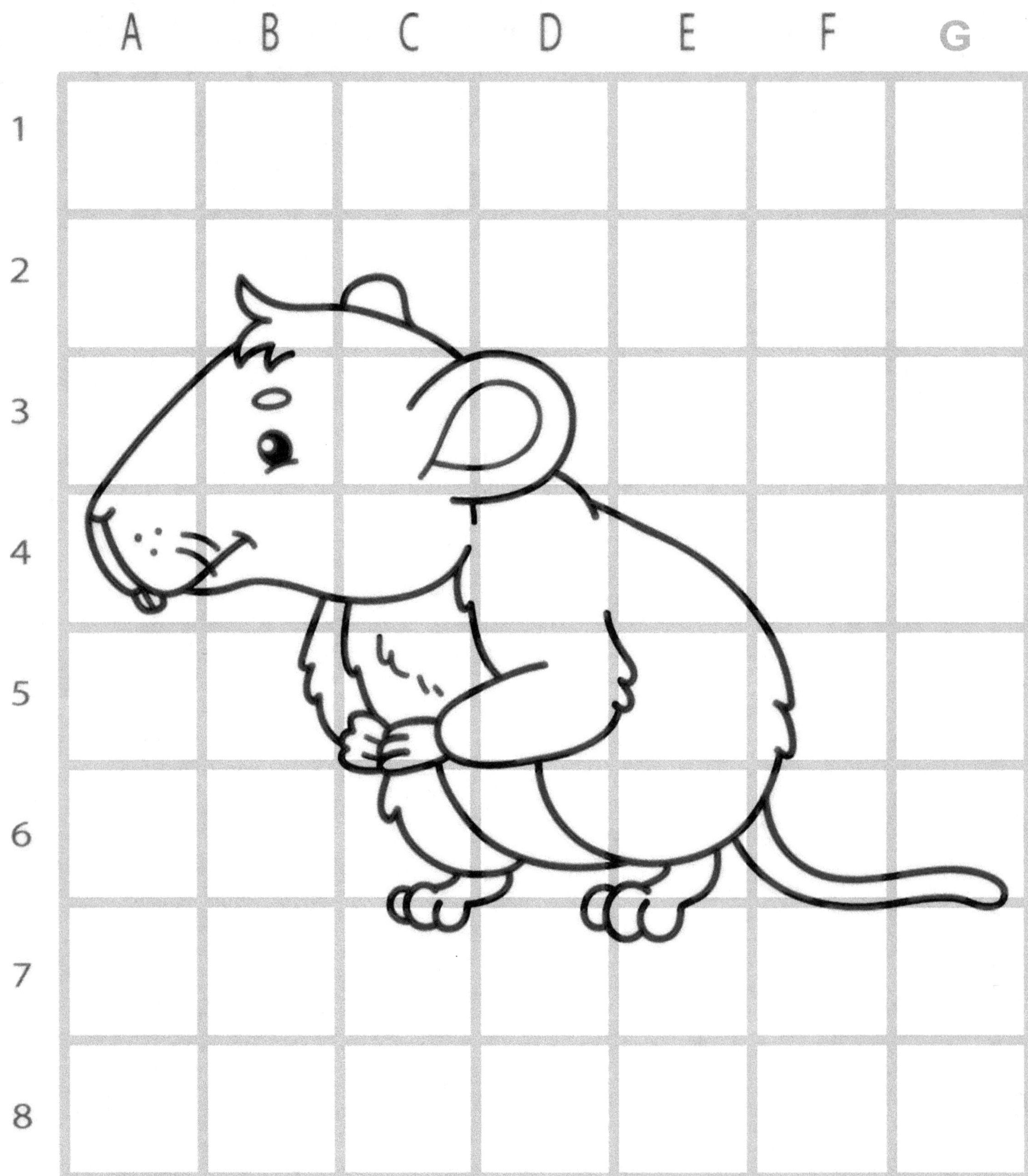

	A	B	C	D	E	F	G
1							
2							
3							
4							
5							
6							
7							
8							

| | A | B | C | D | E | F | G |

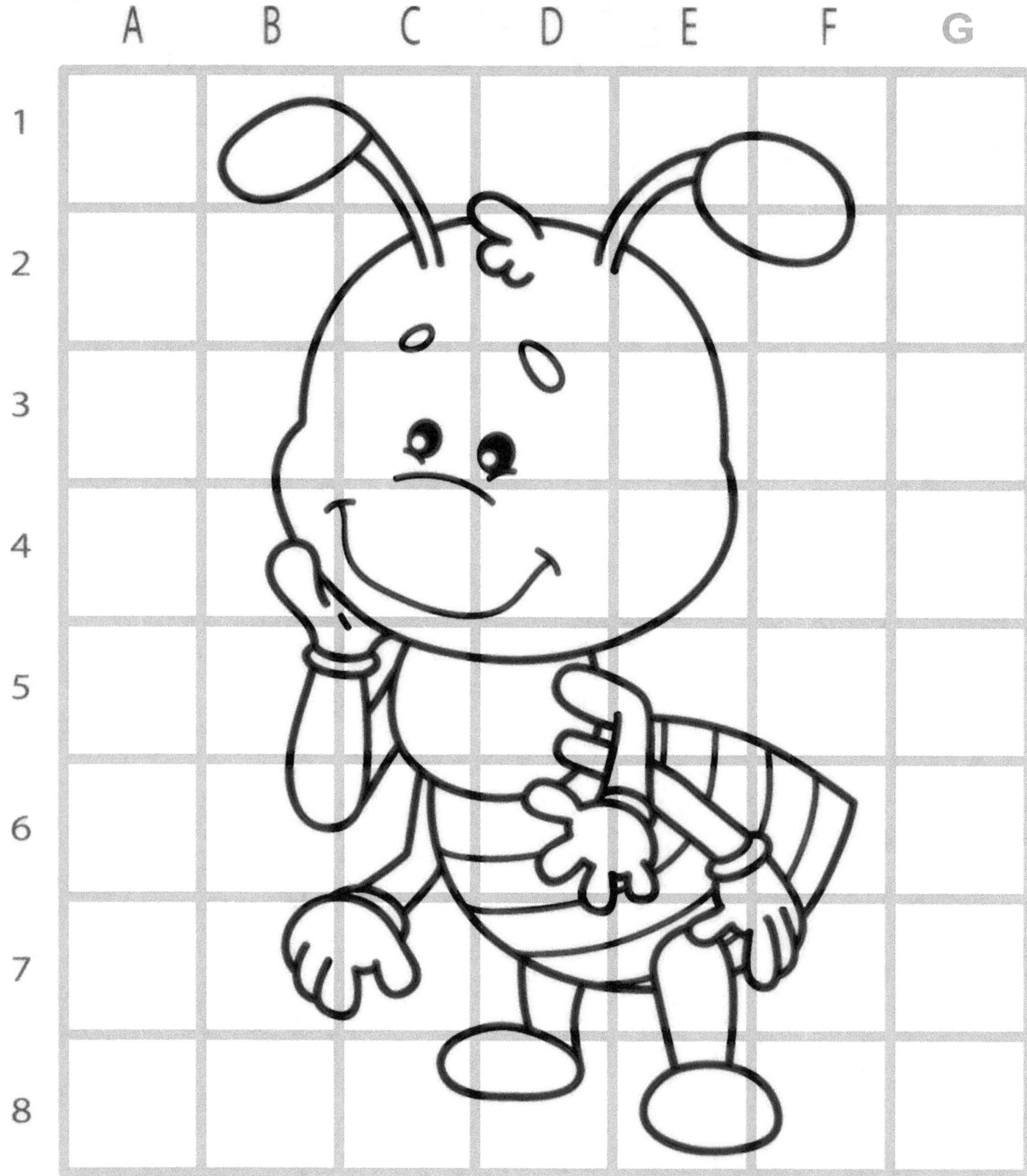

	A	B	C	D	E	F	G
1							
2							
3							
4							
5							
6							
7							
8							

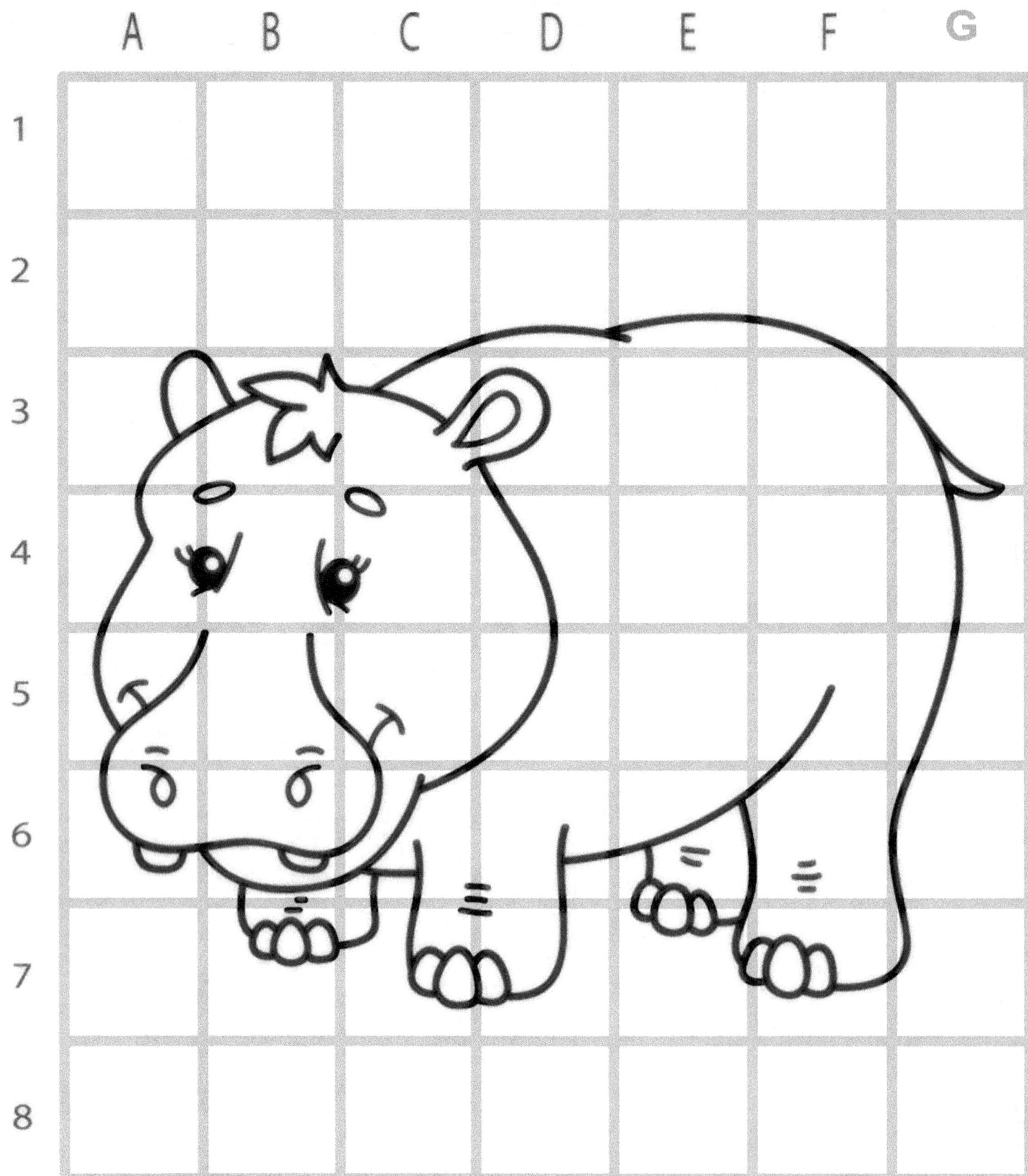

A B C D E F G
1
2
3
4
5
6
7
8

	A	B	C	D	E	F	G
1							
2							
3							
4							
5							
6							
7							
8							

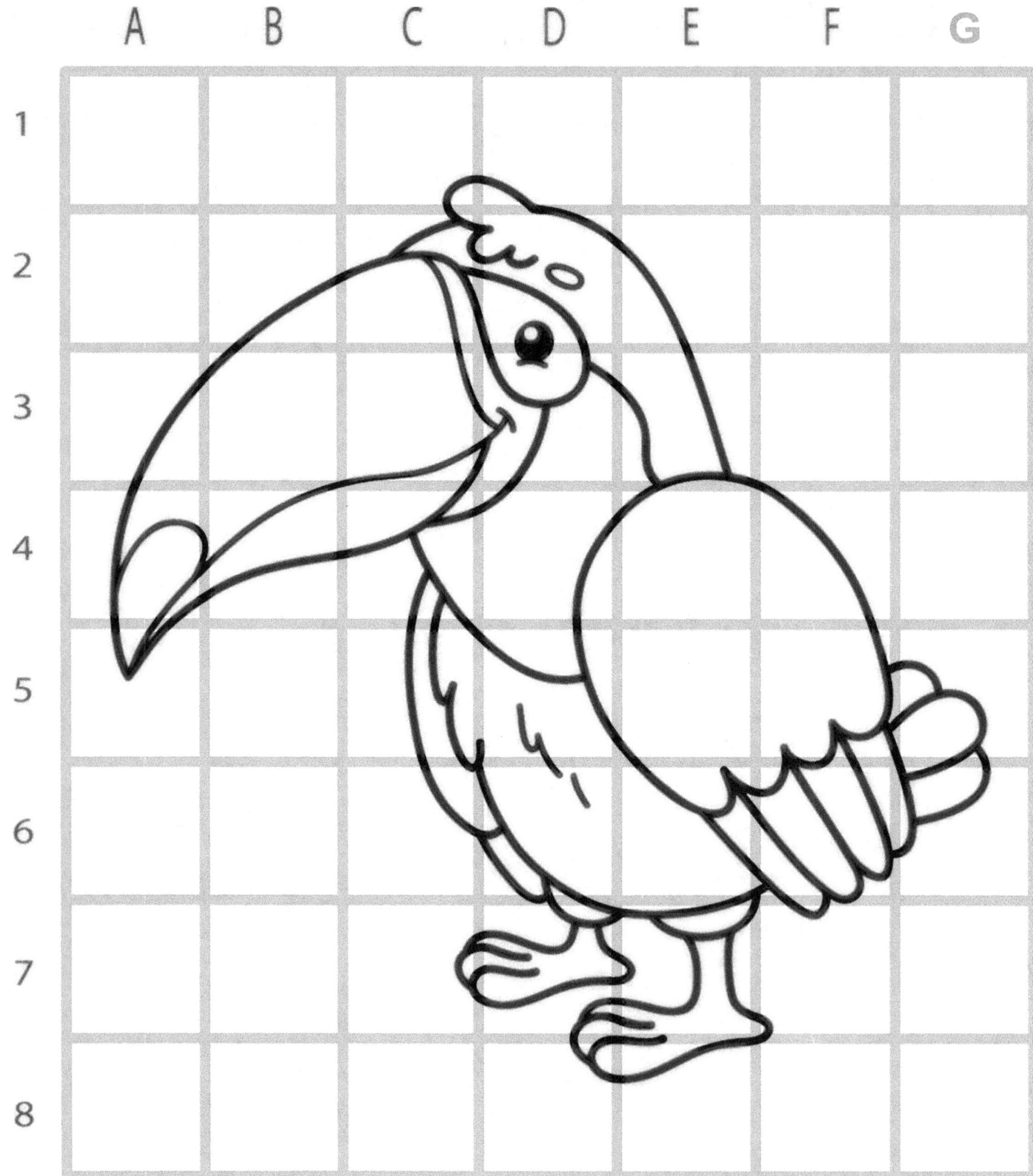

A B C D E F G
1
2
3
4
5
6
7
8

	A	B	C	D	E	F	G
1							
2							
3							
4							
5							
6							
7							
8							

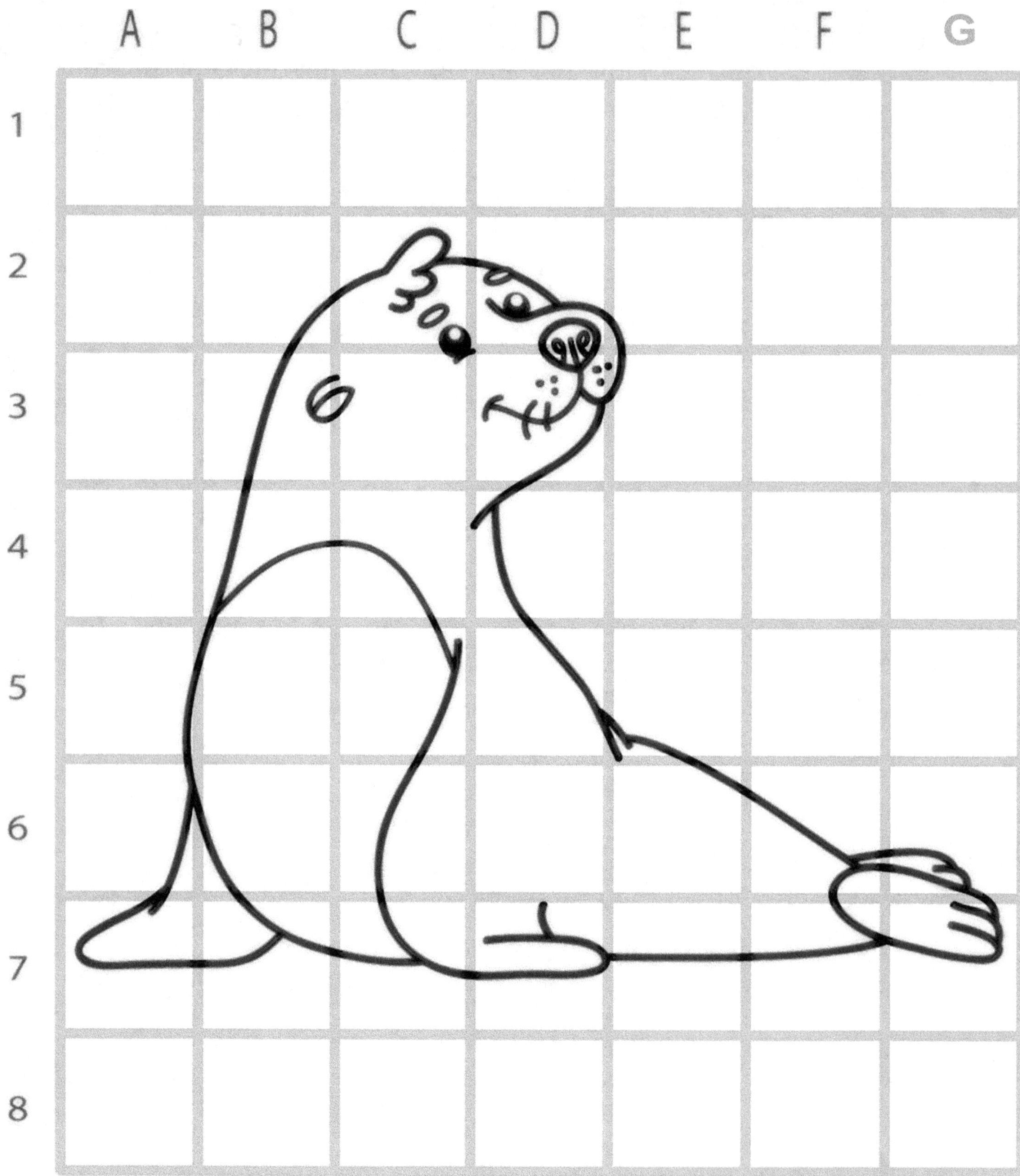

A   B   C   D   E   F   G
1
2
3
4
5
6
7
8

	A	B	C	D	E	F	G
1							
2							
3							
4							
5							
6							
7							
8							

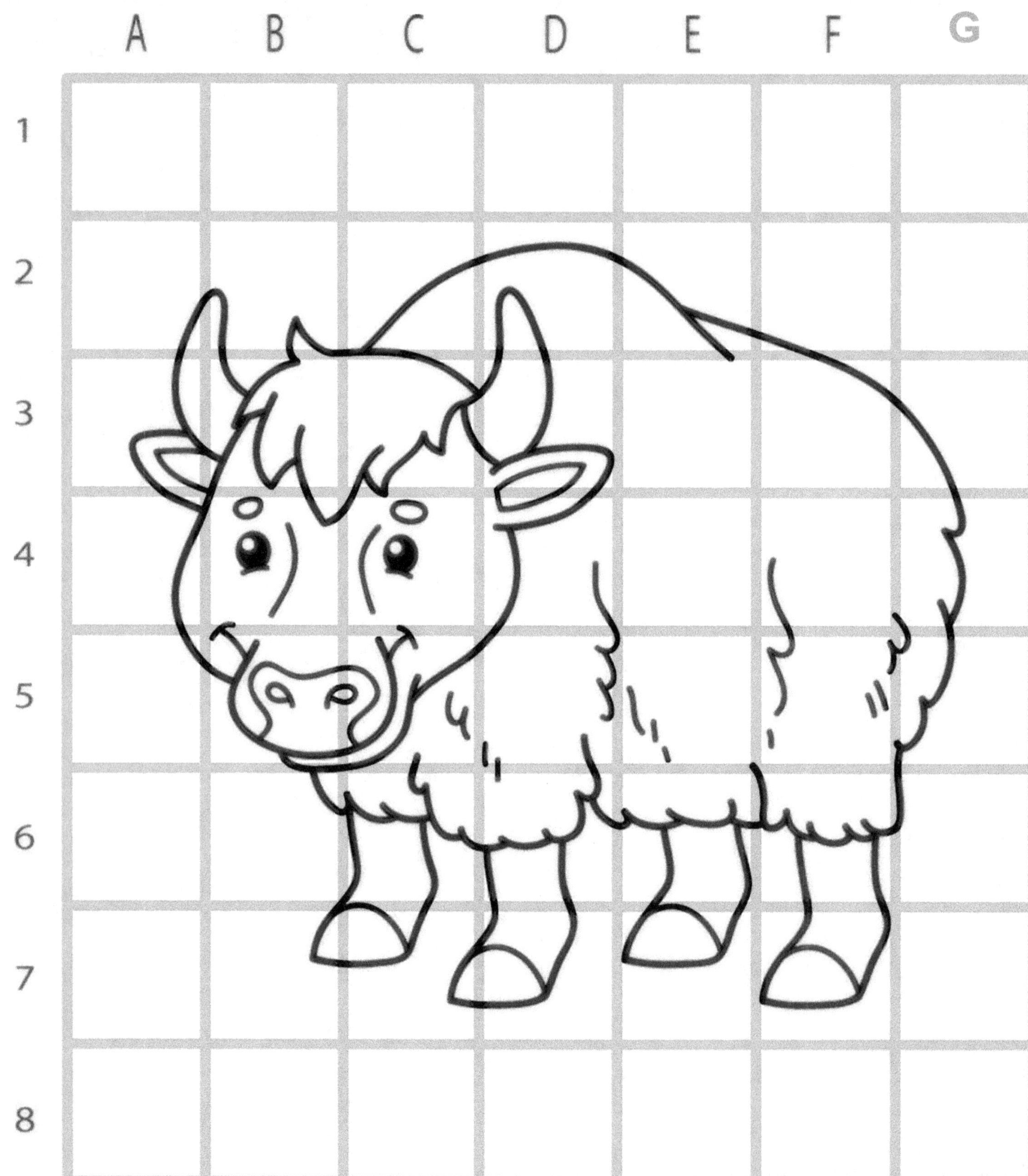

	A	B	C	D	E	F	G
1							
2							
3							
4							
5							
6							
7							
8							

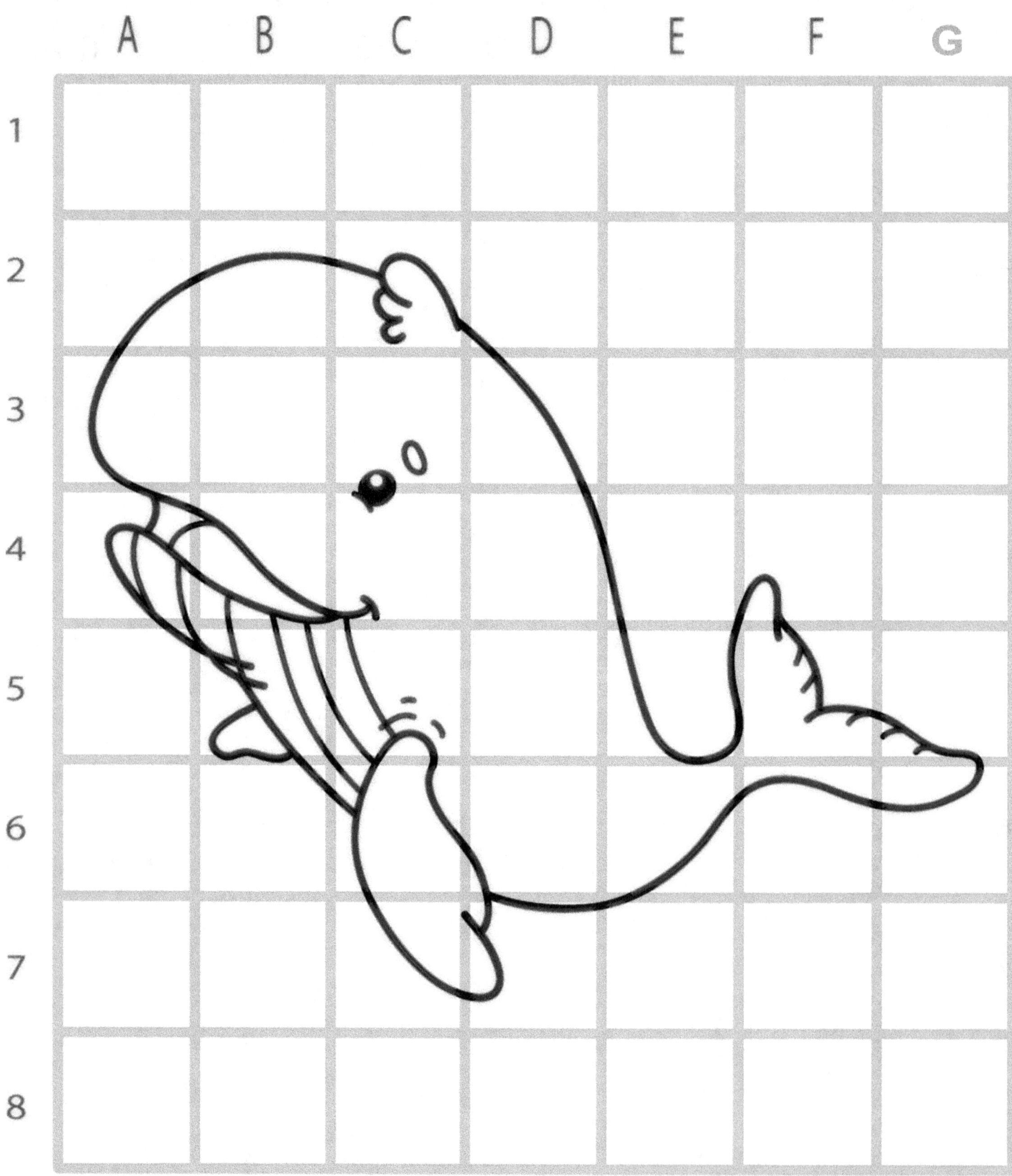

A B C D E F G
1
2
3
4
5
6
7
8

	A	B	C	D	E	F	G
1							
2							
3							
4							
5							
6							
7							
8							

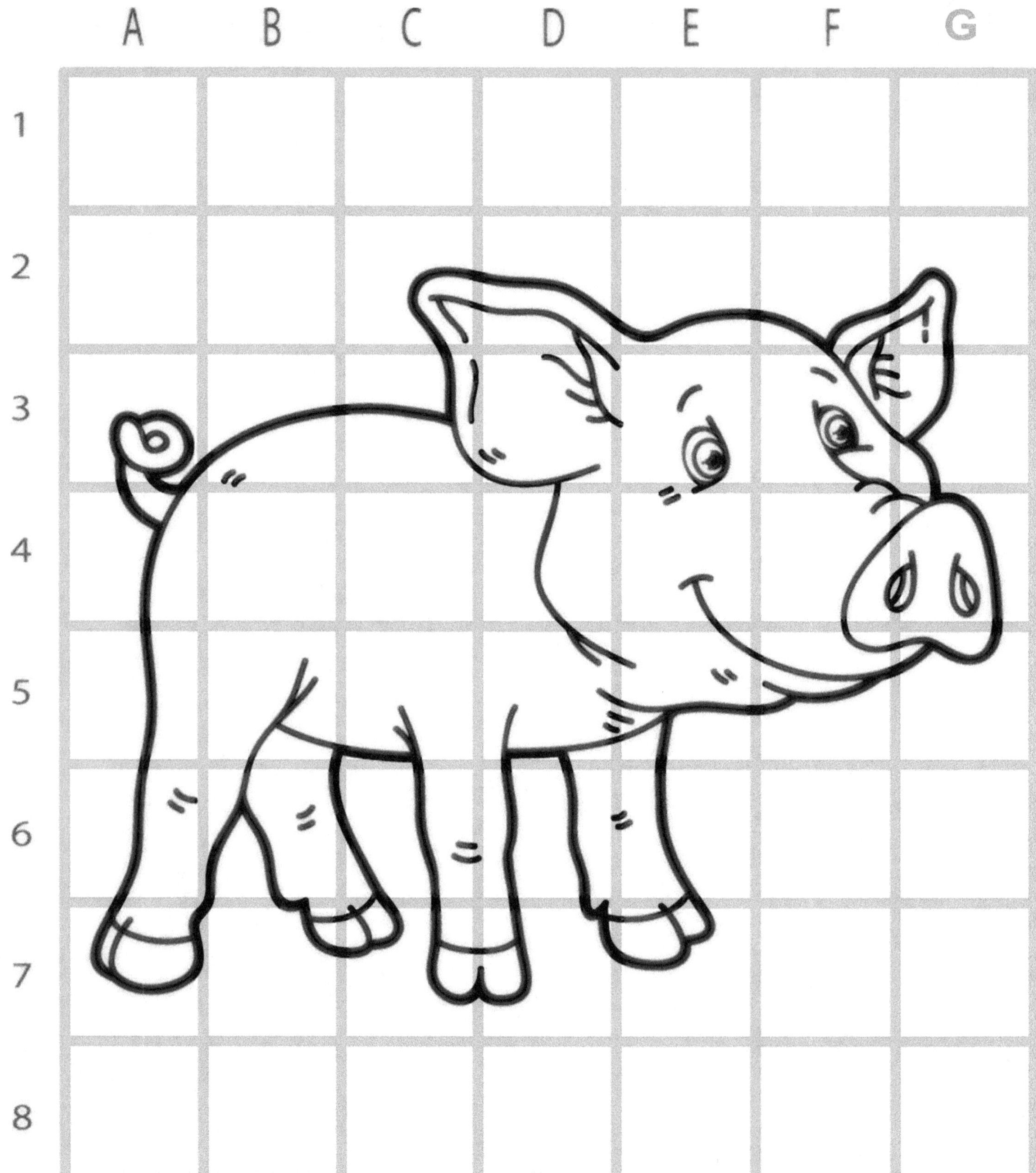

A B C D E F G
1
2
3
4
5
6
7
8

	A	B	C	D	E	F	G
1							
2							
3							
4							
5							
6							
7							
8							

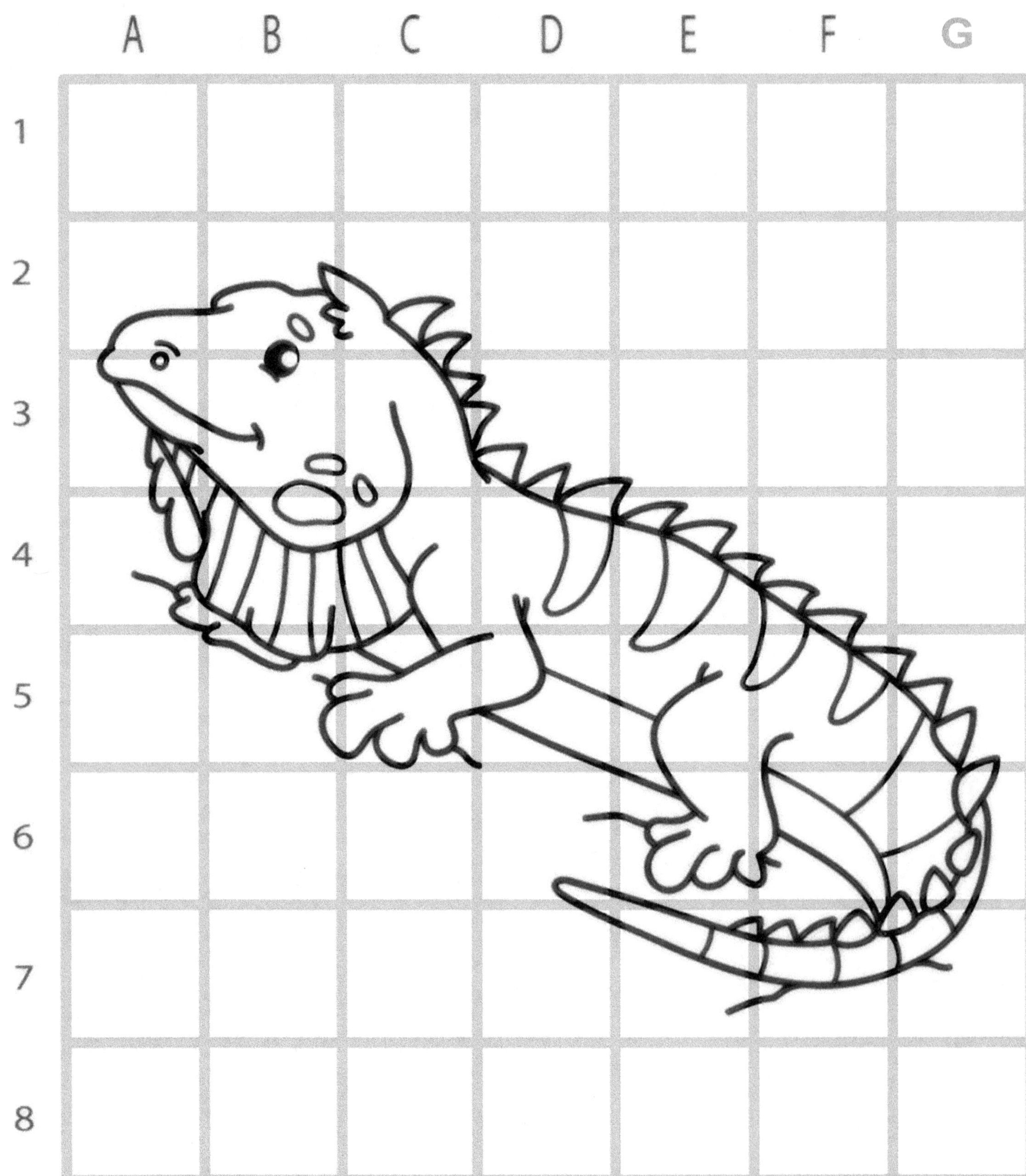

A   B   C   D   E   F   G
1
2
3
4
5
6
7
8

	A	B	C	D	E	F	G
1							
2							
3							
4							
5							
6							
7							
8							

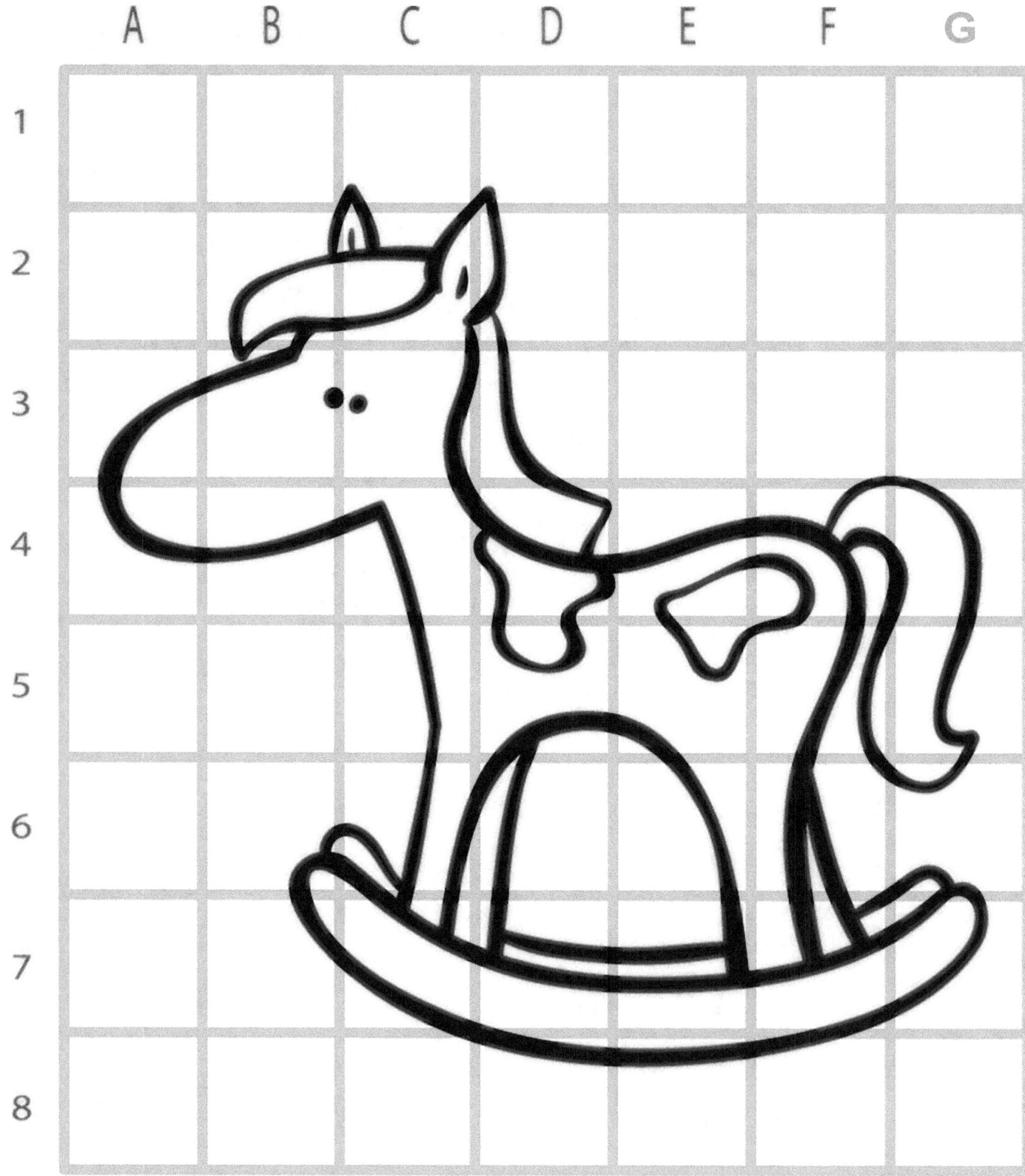

	A	B	C	D	E	F	G
1							
2							
3							
4							
5							
6							
7							
8							

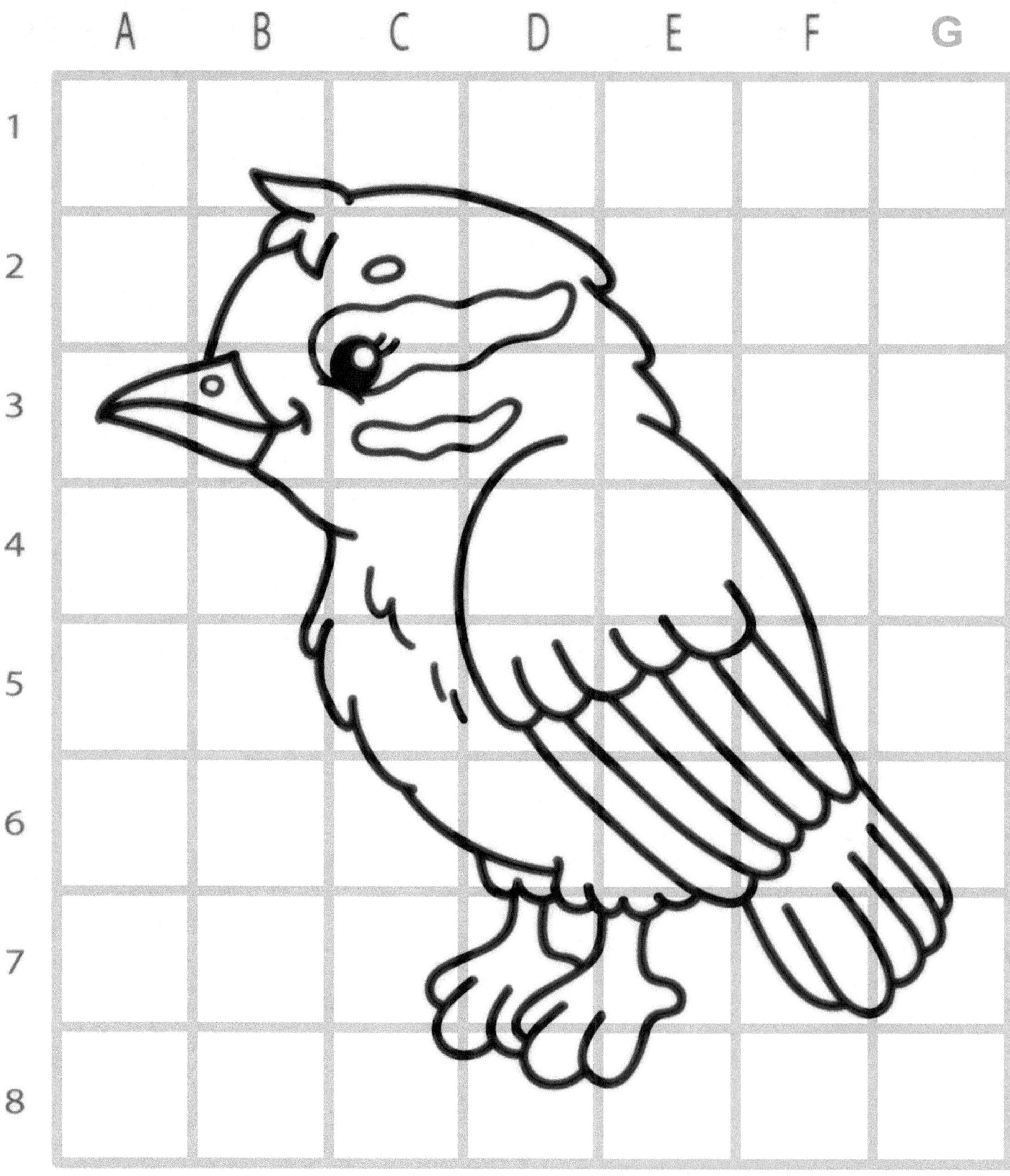

	A	B	C	D	E	F	G
1							
2							
3							
4							
5							
6							
7							
8							

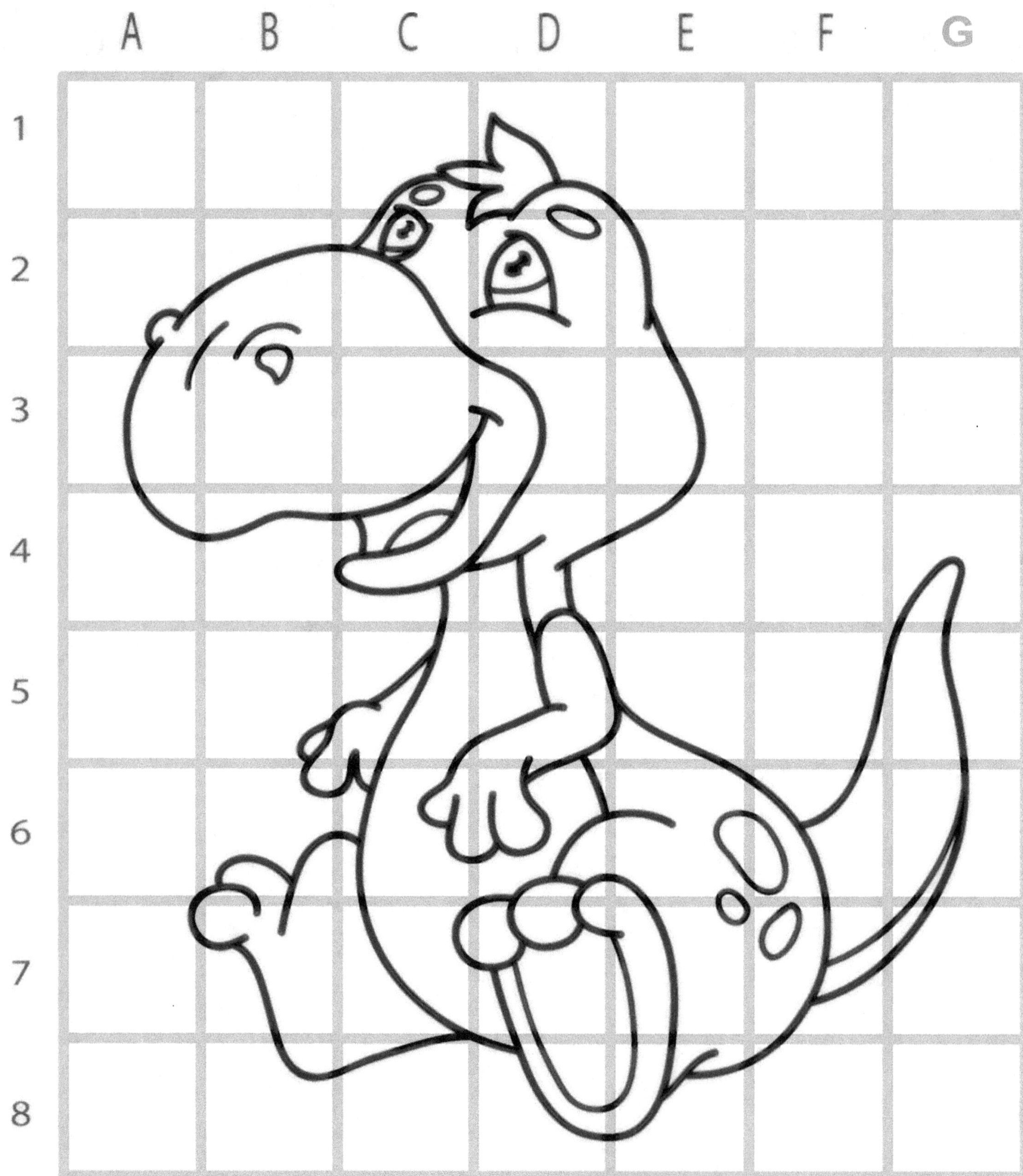

A B C D E F G
1 2 3 4 5 6 7 8

	A	B	C	D	E	F	G
1							
2							
3							
4							
5							
6							
7							
8							

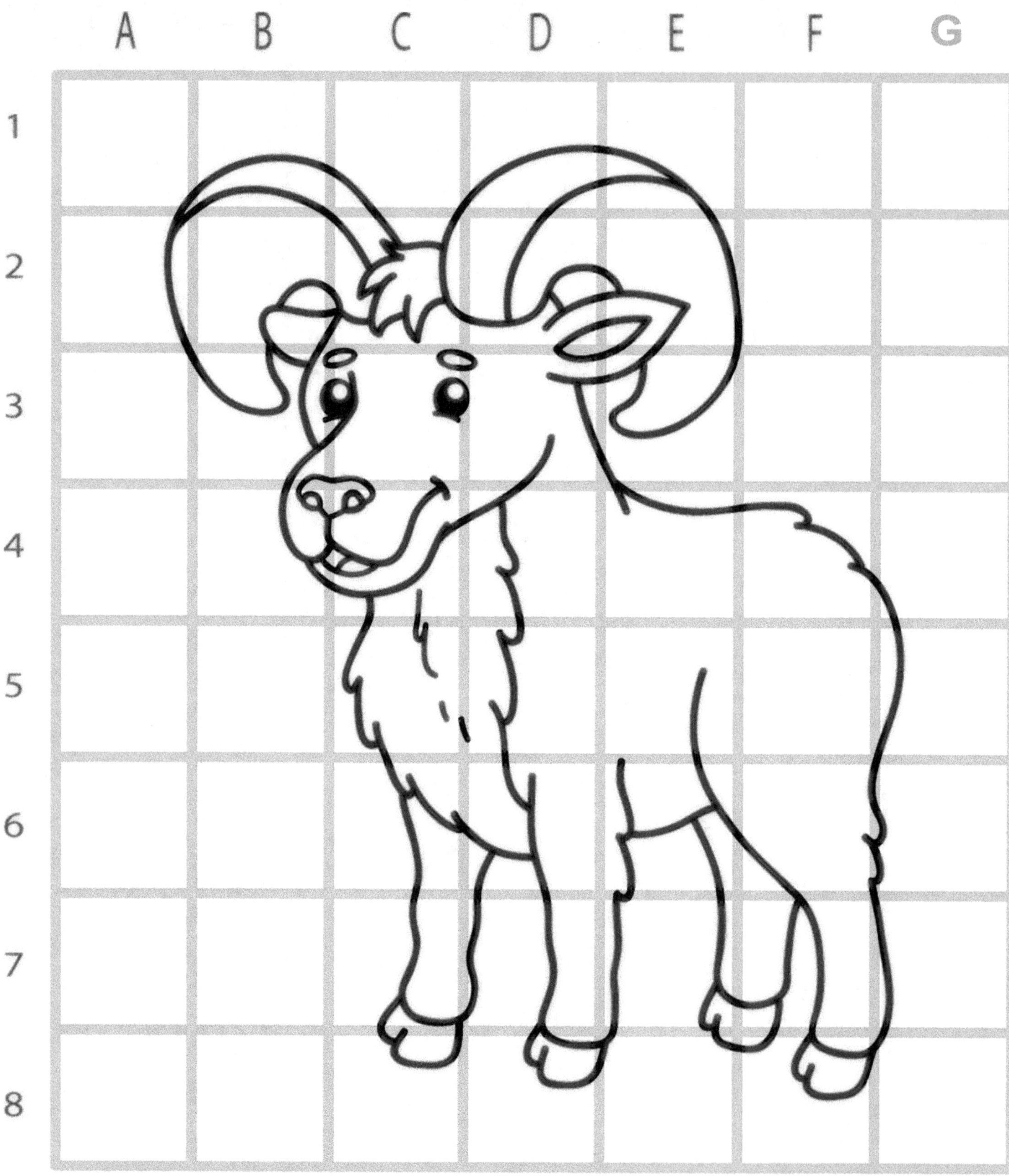

A B C D E F G
1
2
3
4
5
6
7
8

	A	B	C	D	E	F	G
1							
2							
3							
4							
5							
6							
7							
8							

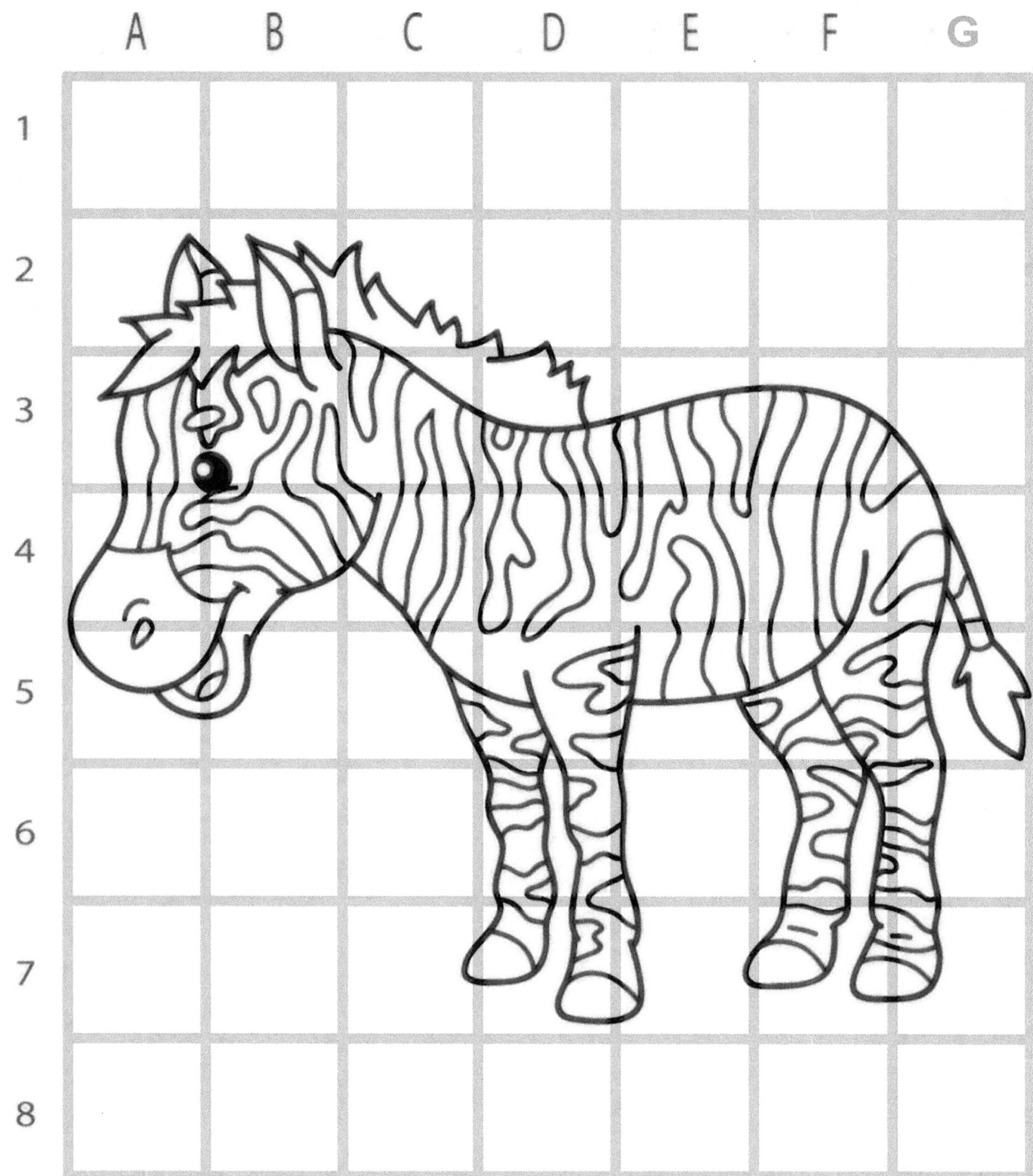
A B C D E F G
1
2
3
4
5
6
7
8

	A	B	C	D	E	F	G
1							
2							
3							
4							
5							
6							
7							
8							

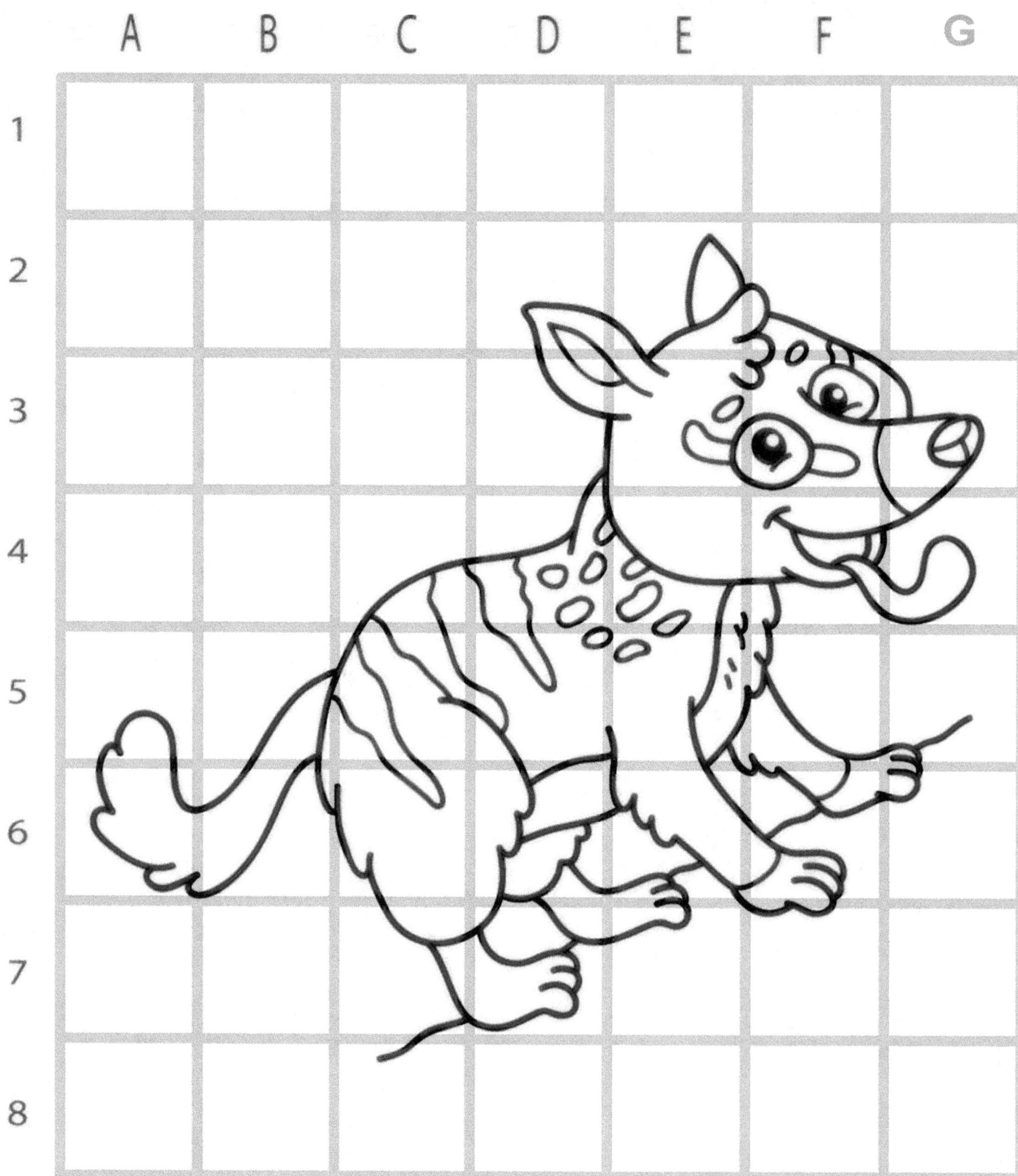

	A	B	C	D	E	F	G
1							
2							
3							
4							
5							
6							
7							
8							

A B C D E F G
1
2
3
4
5
6
7
8

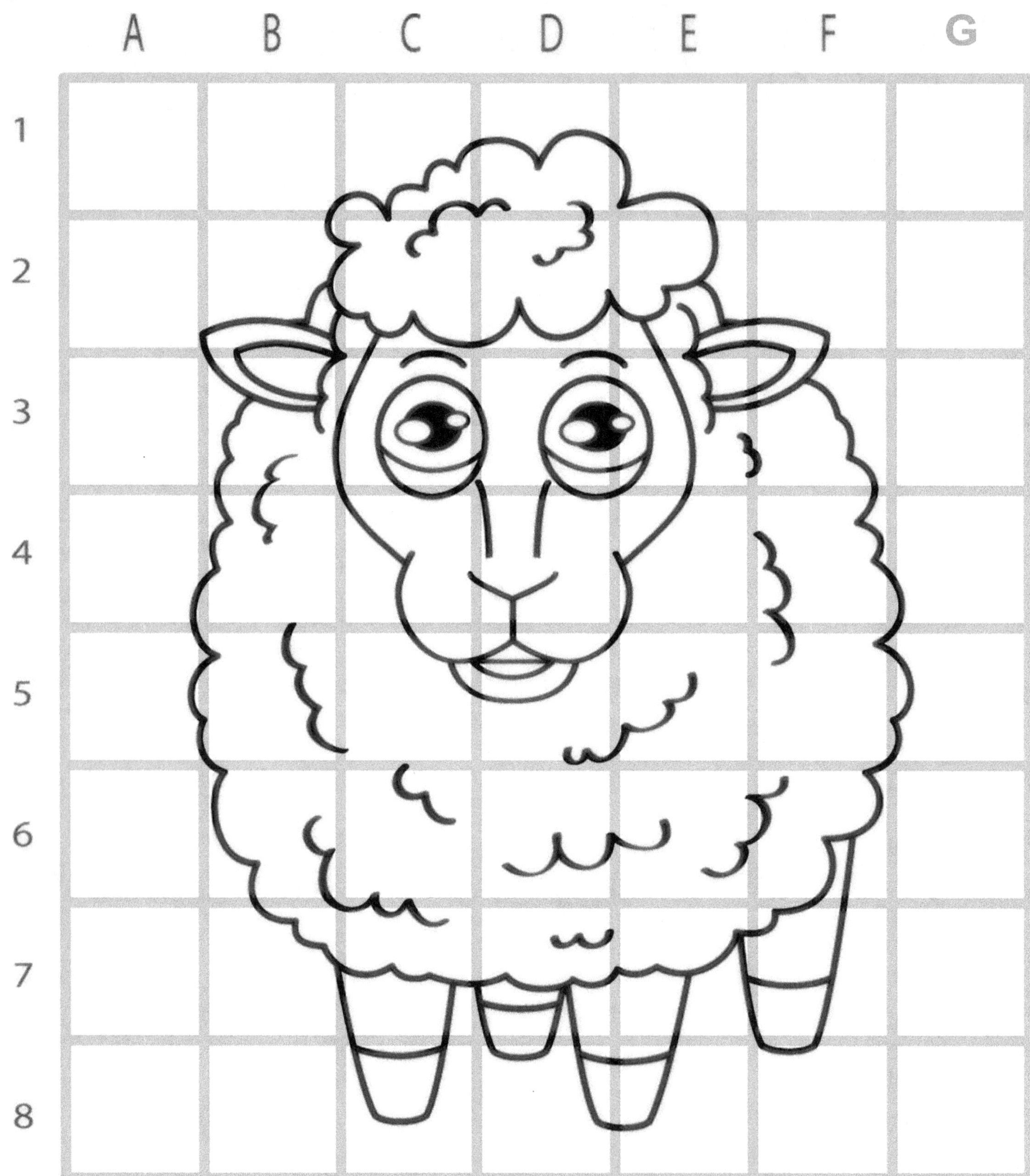

	A	B	C	D	E	F	G
1							
2							
3							
4							
5							
6							
7							
8							

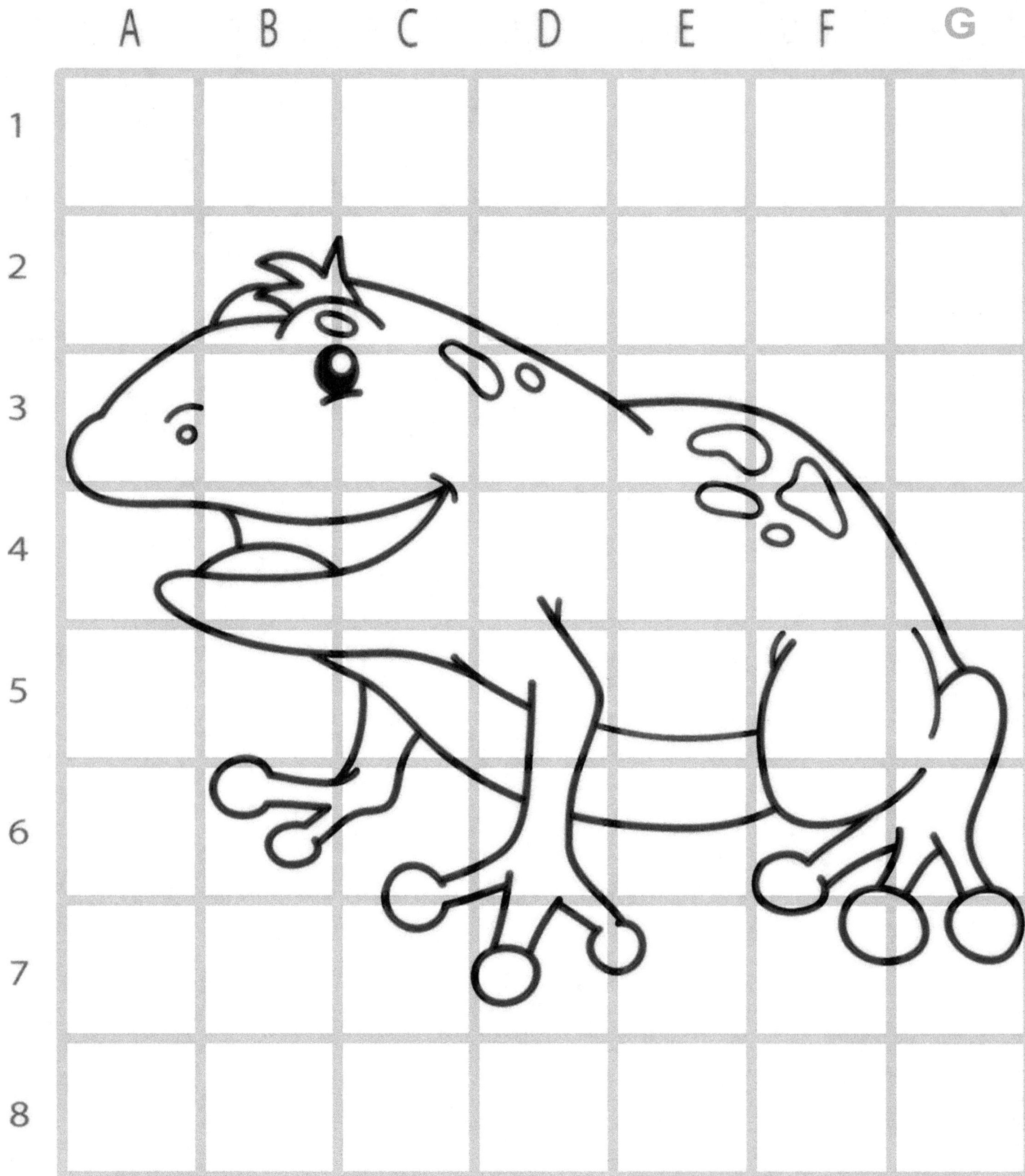

A B C D E F G
1
2
3
4
5
6
7
8

	A	B	C	D	E	F	G
1							
2							
3							
4							
5							
6							
7							
8							

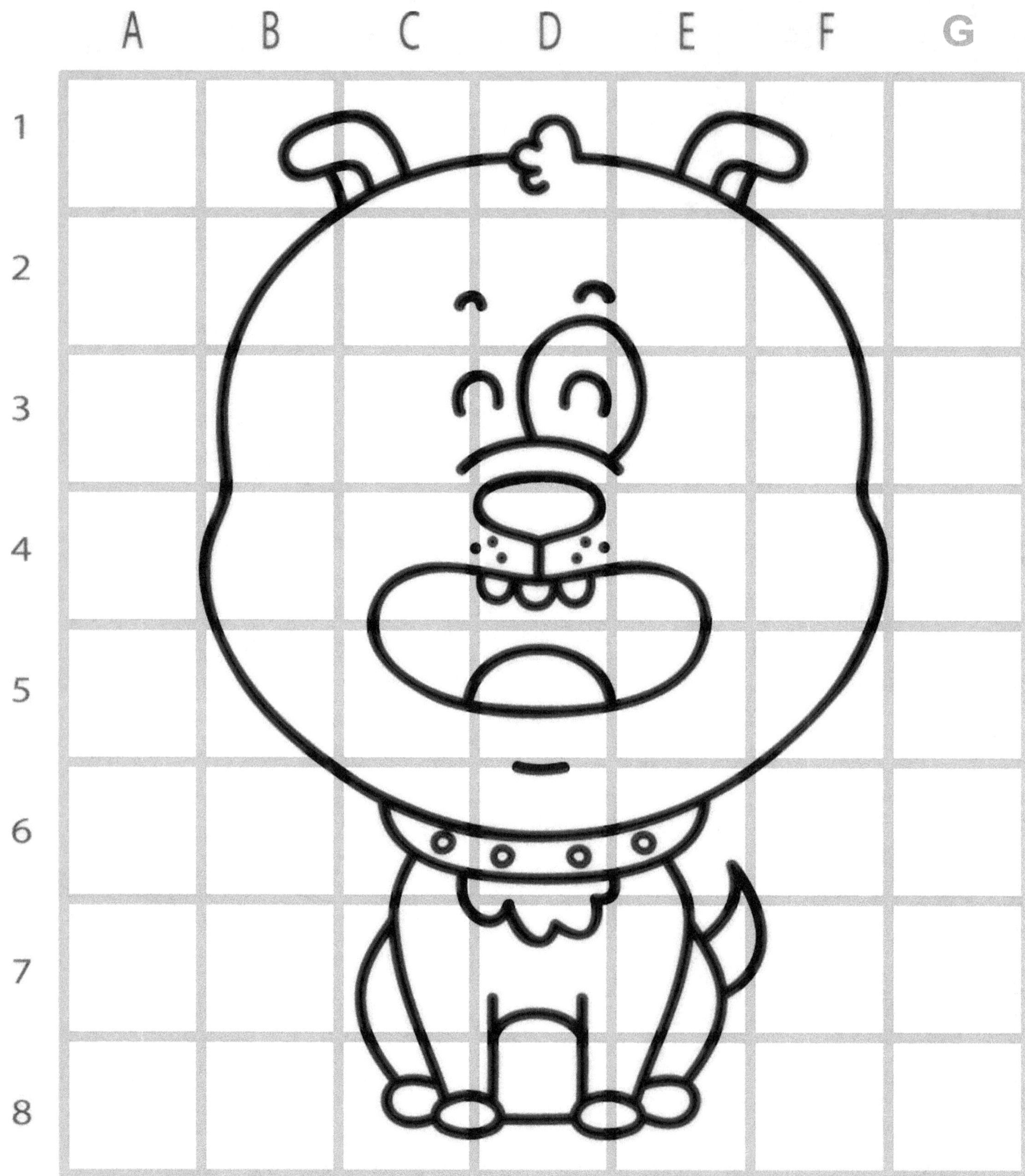

	A	B	C	D	E	F	G
1							
2							
3							
4							
5							
6							
7							
8							

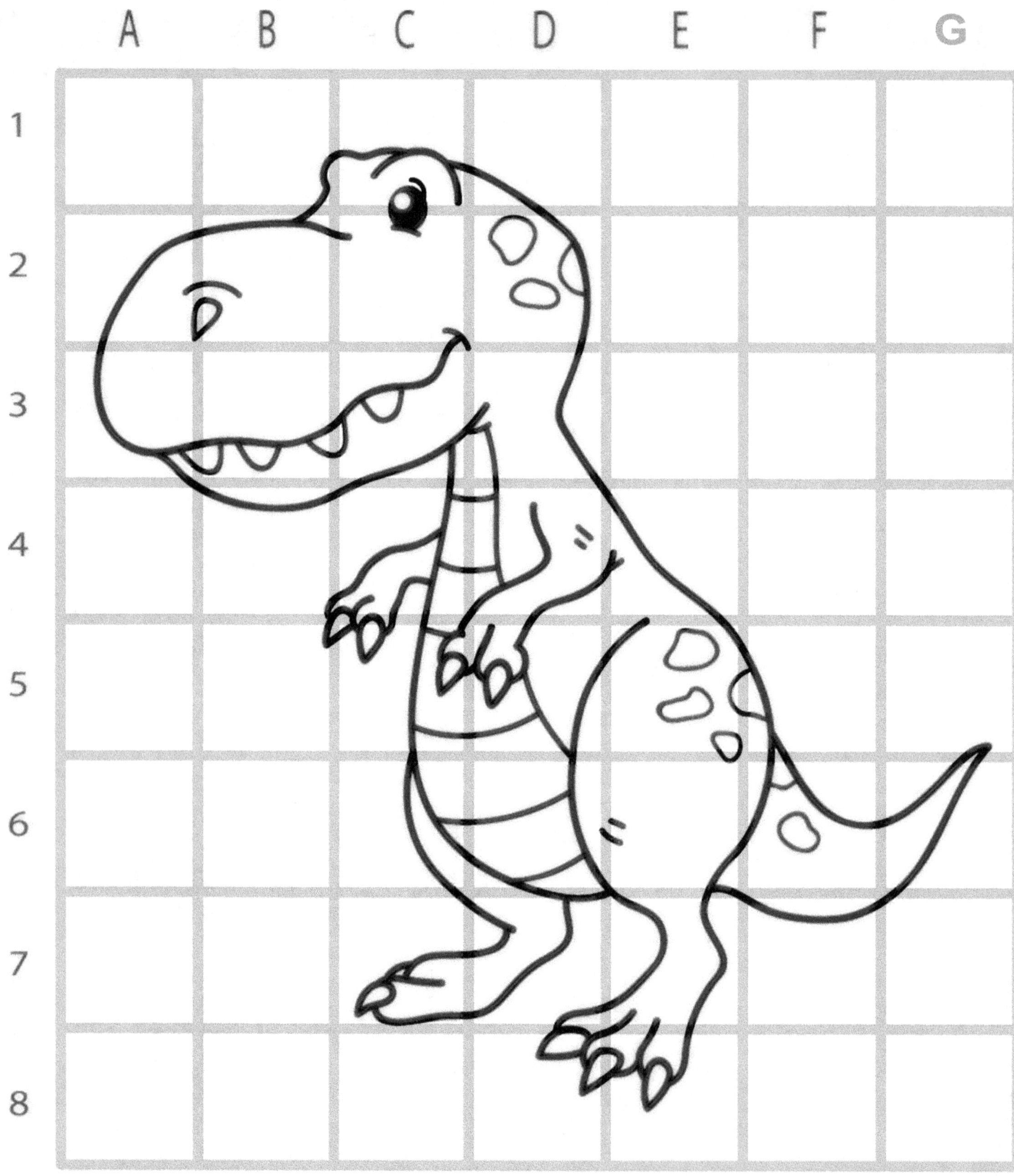

A B C D E F G
1
2
3
4
5
6
7
8

	A	B	C	D	E	F	G
1							
2							
3							
4							
5							
6							
7							
8							

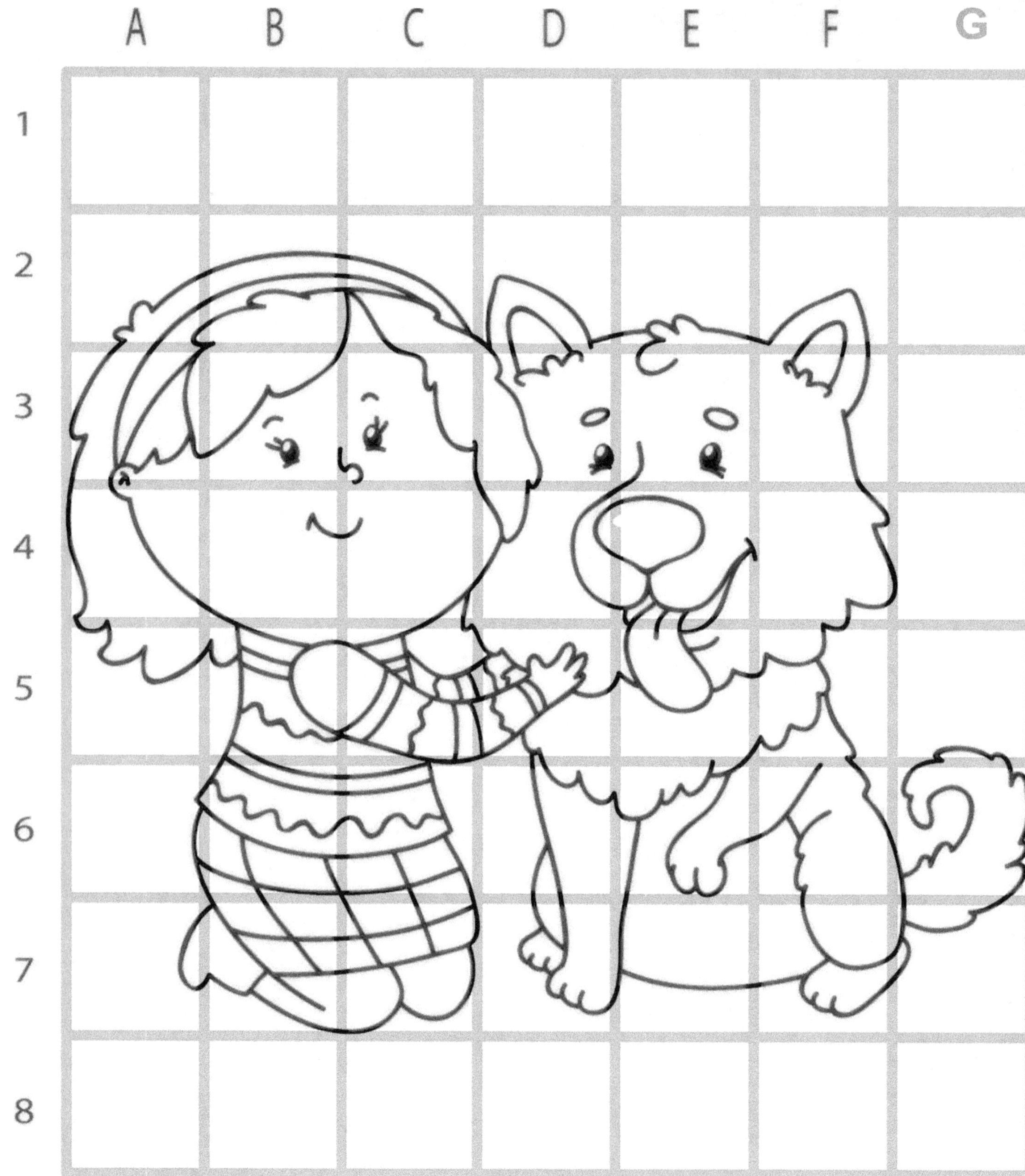

A B C D E F G
1
2
3
4
5
6
7
8

	A	B	C	D	E	F	G
1							
2							
3							
4							
5							
6							
7							
8							

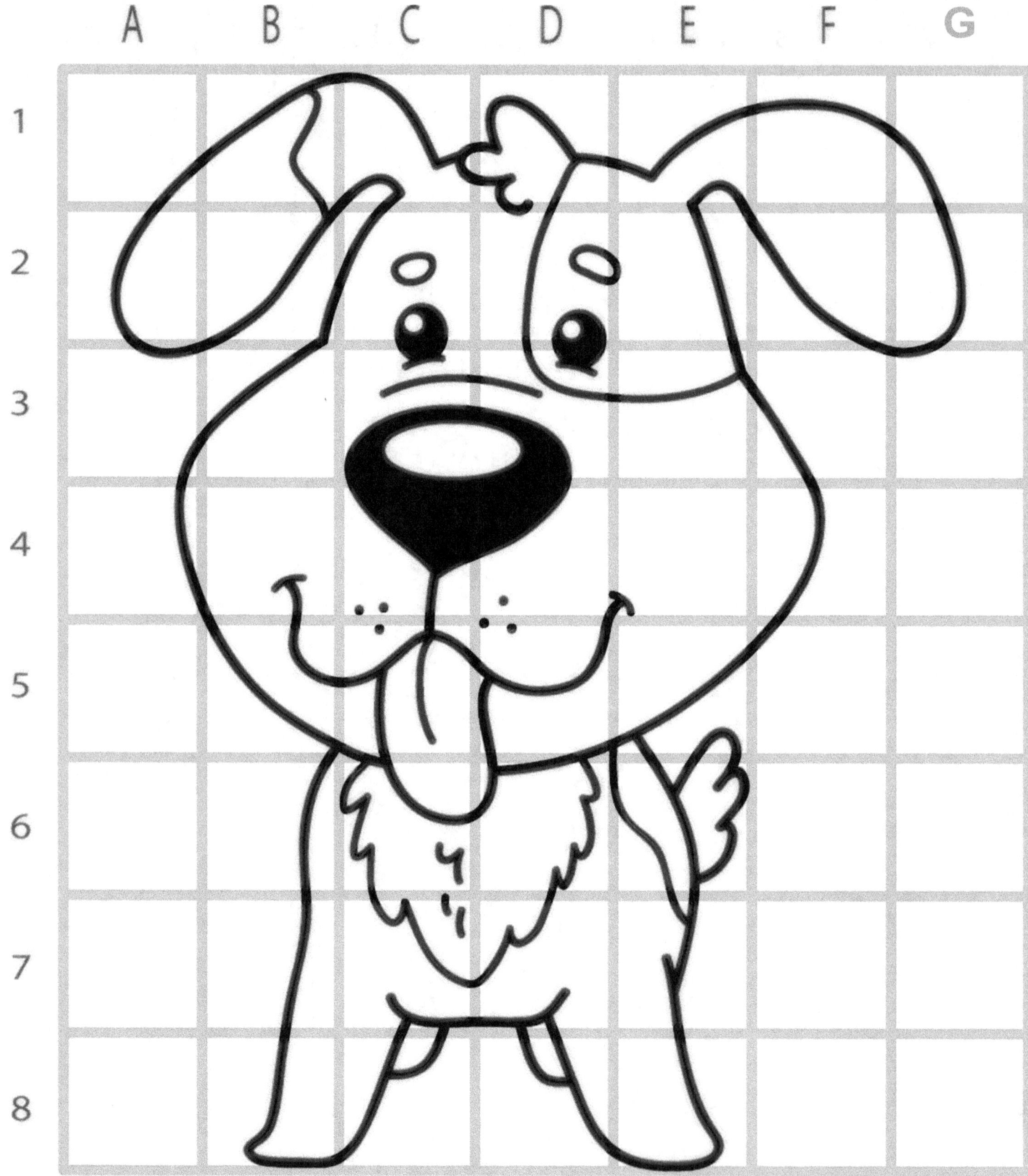

A B C D E F G
1
2
3
4
5
6
7
8

	A	B	C	D	E	F	G
1							
2							
3							
4							
5							
6							
7							
8							

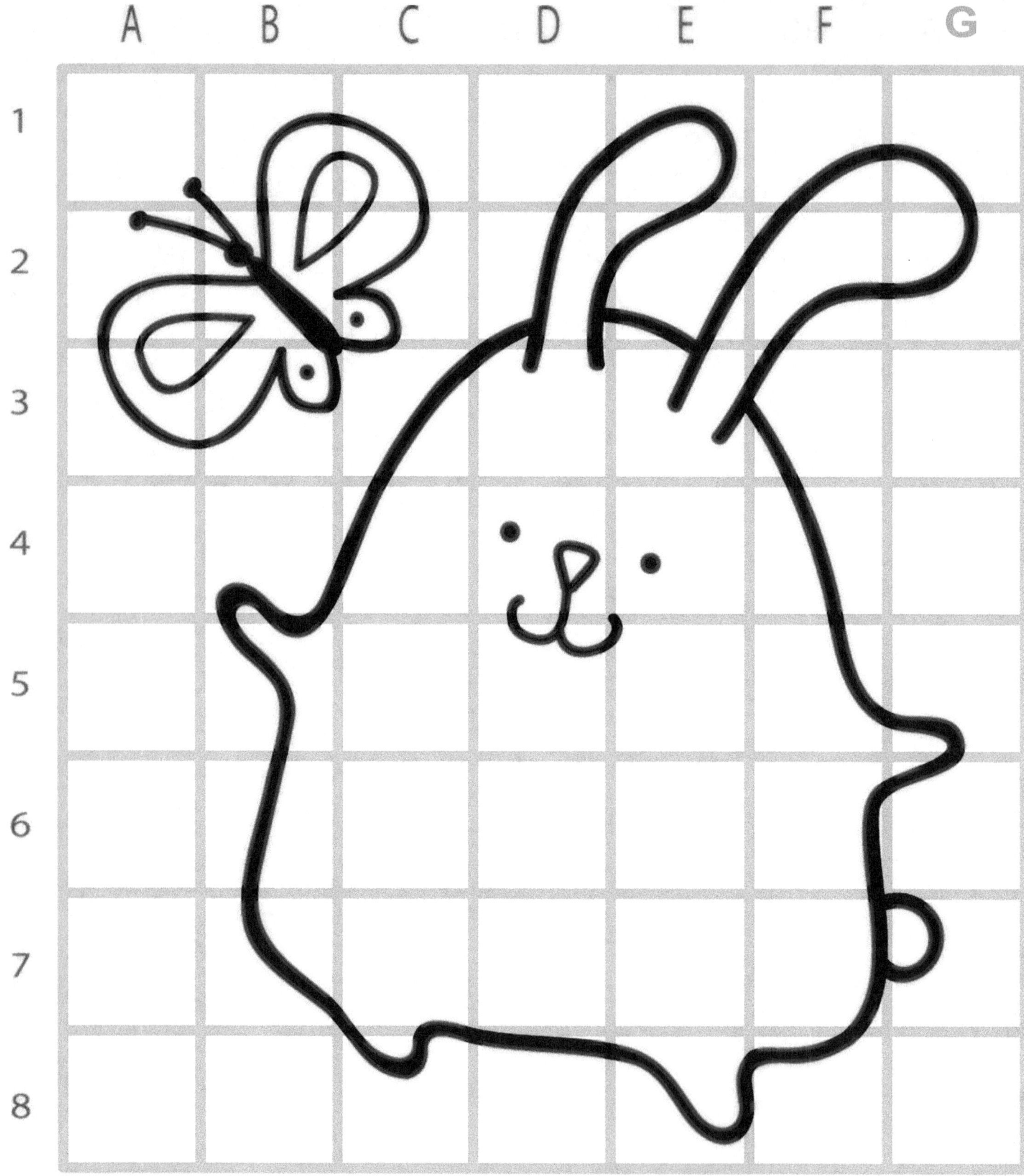
A B C D E F G
1 2 3 4 5 6 7 8

	A	B	C	D	E	F	G
1							
2							
3							
4							
5							
6							
7							
8							

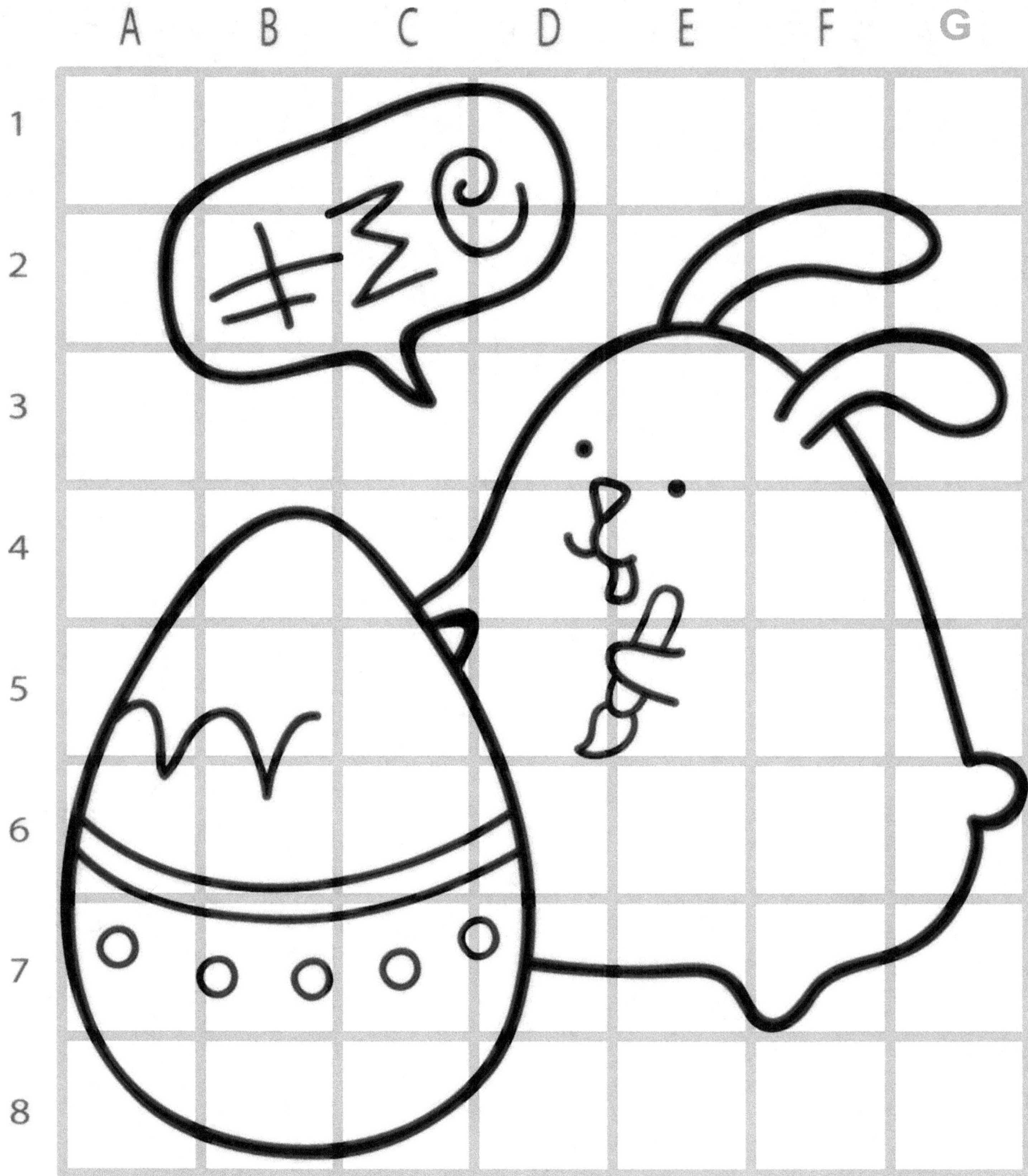

	A	B	C	D	E	F	G
1							
2							
3							
4							
5							
6							
7							
8							

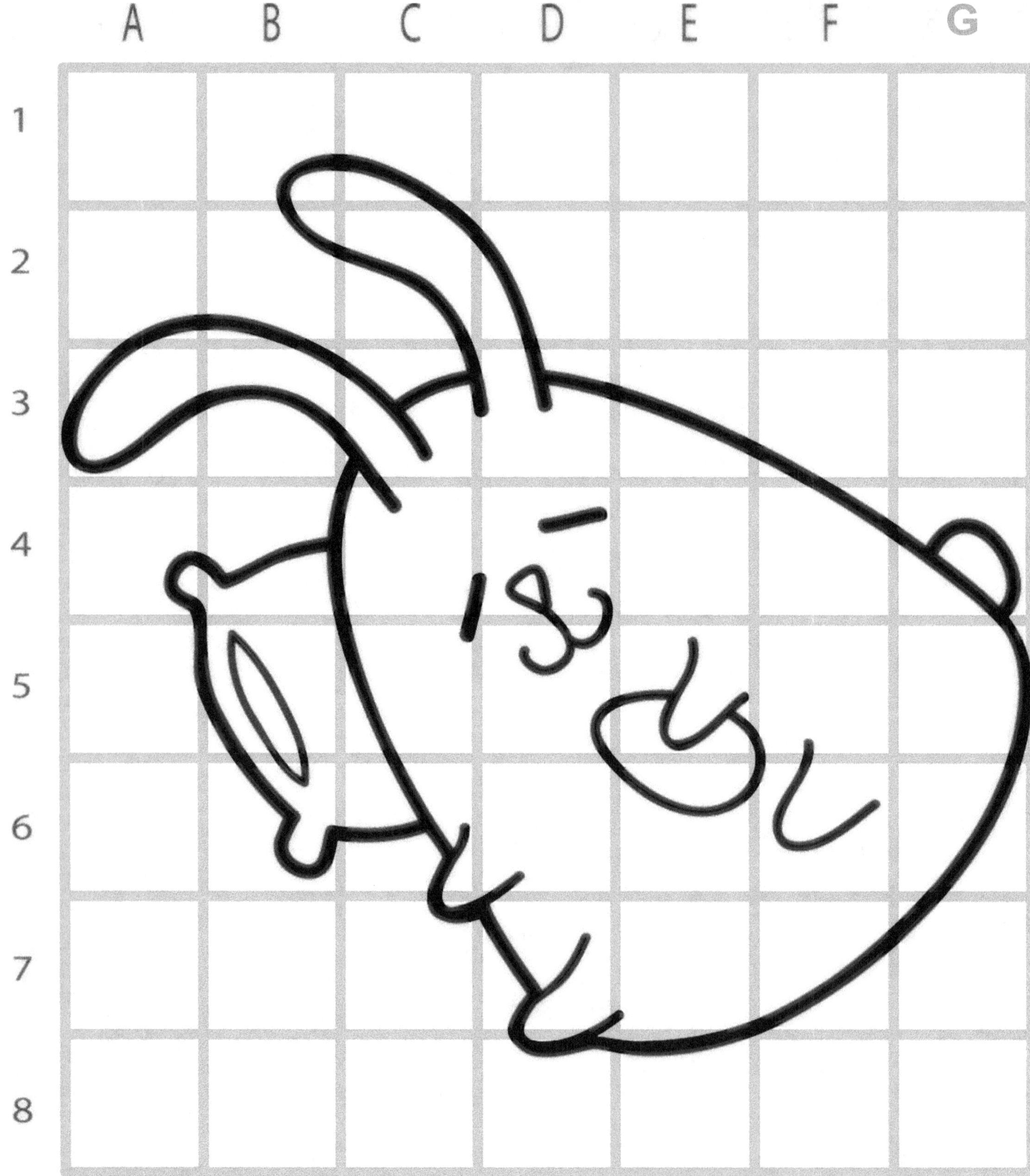

	A	B	C	D	E	F	G
1							
2							
3							
4							
5							
6							
7							
8							

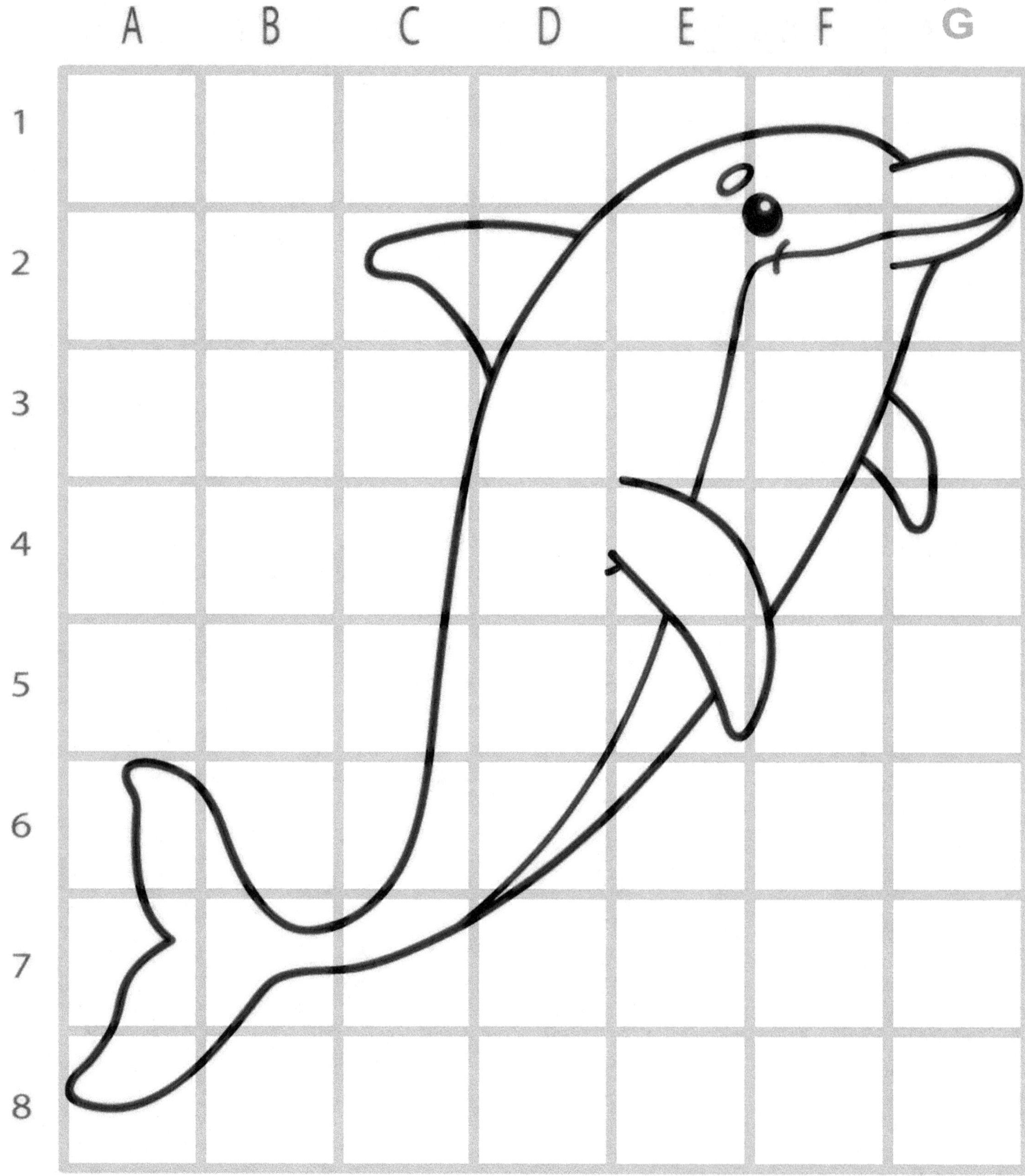
A B C D E F G
1
2
3
4
5
6
7
8

	A	B	C	D	E	F	G
1							
2							
3							
4							
5							
6							
7							
8							

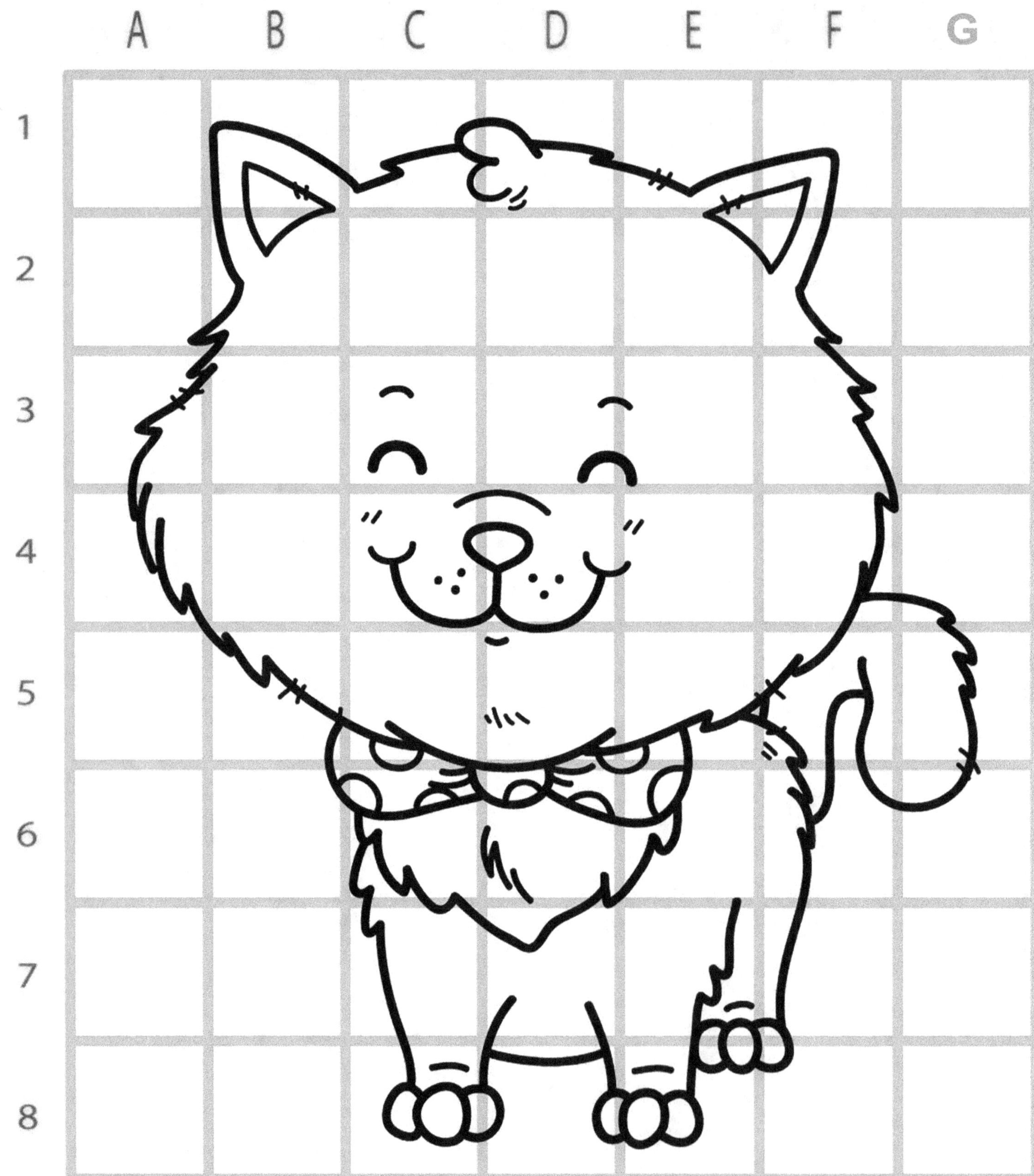
A B C D E F G
1
2
3
4
5
6
7
8

	A	B	C	D	E	F	G
1							
2							
3							
4							
5							
6							
7							
8							

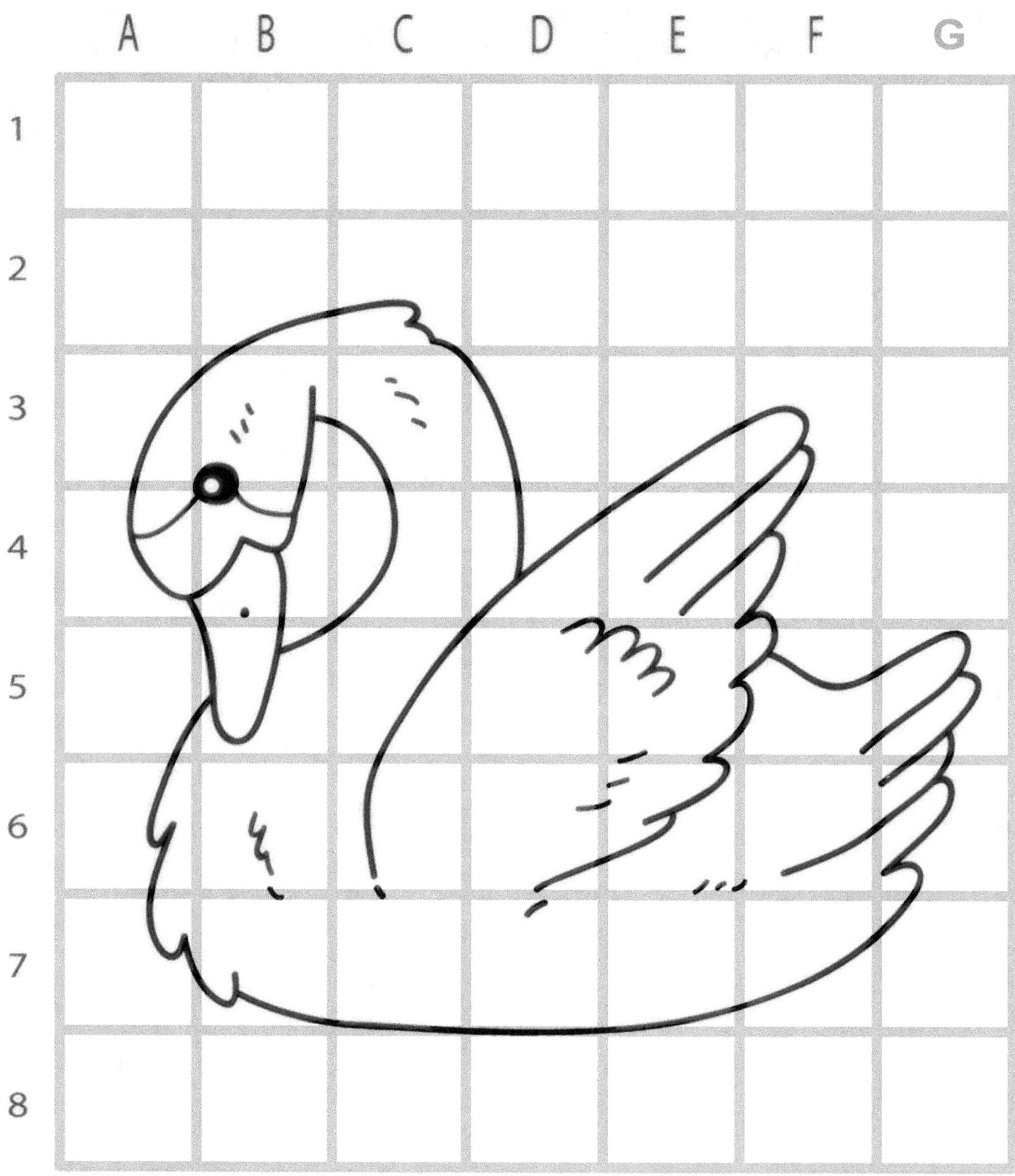

A B C D E F G
1
2
3
4
5
6
7
8

	A	B	C	D	E	F	G
1							
2							
3							
4							
5							
6							
7							
8							

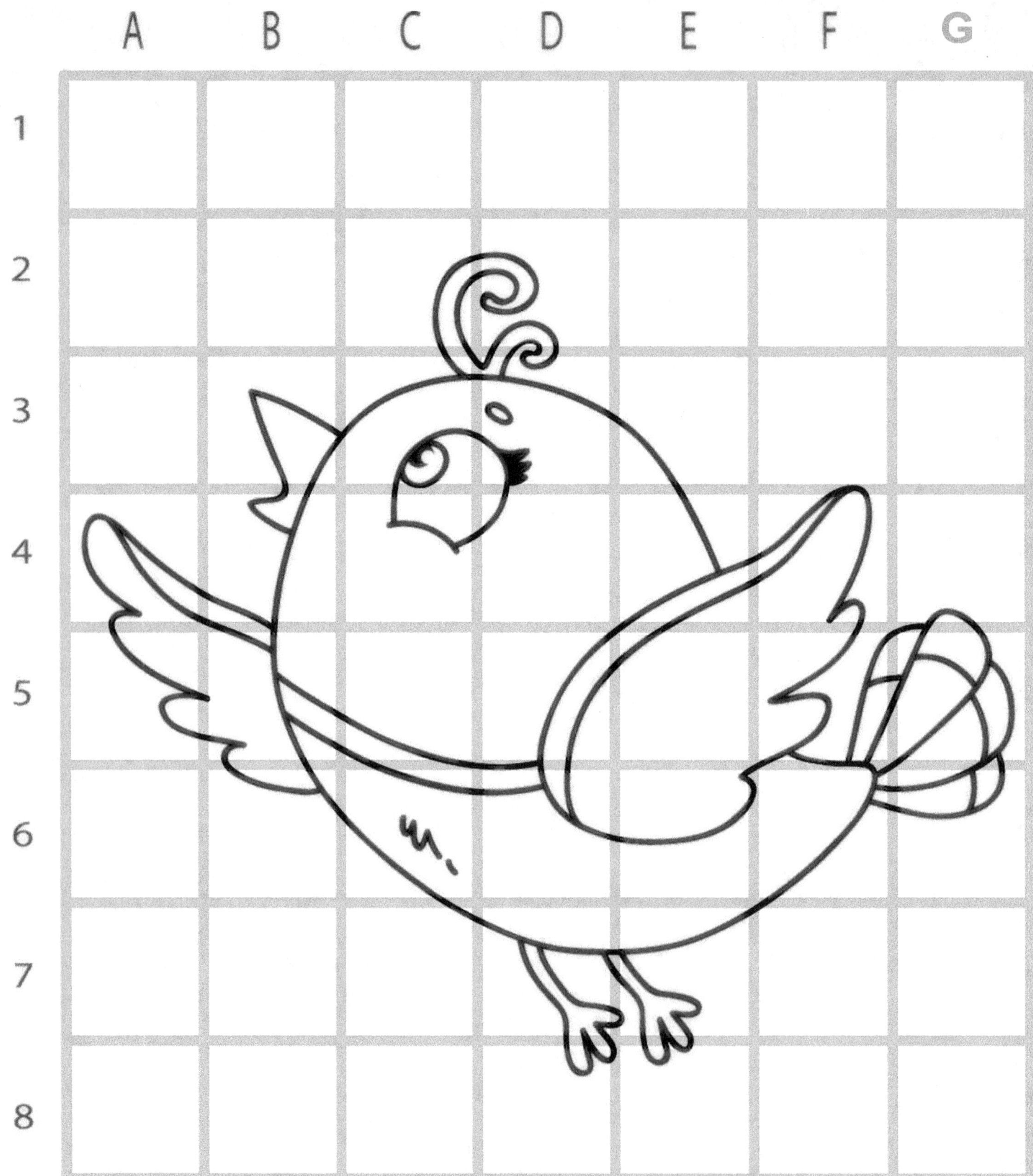

A B C D E F G
1
2
3
4
5
6
7
8

	A	B	C	D	E	F	G
1							
2							
3							
4							
5							
6							
7							
8							

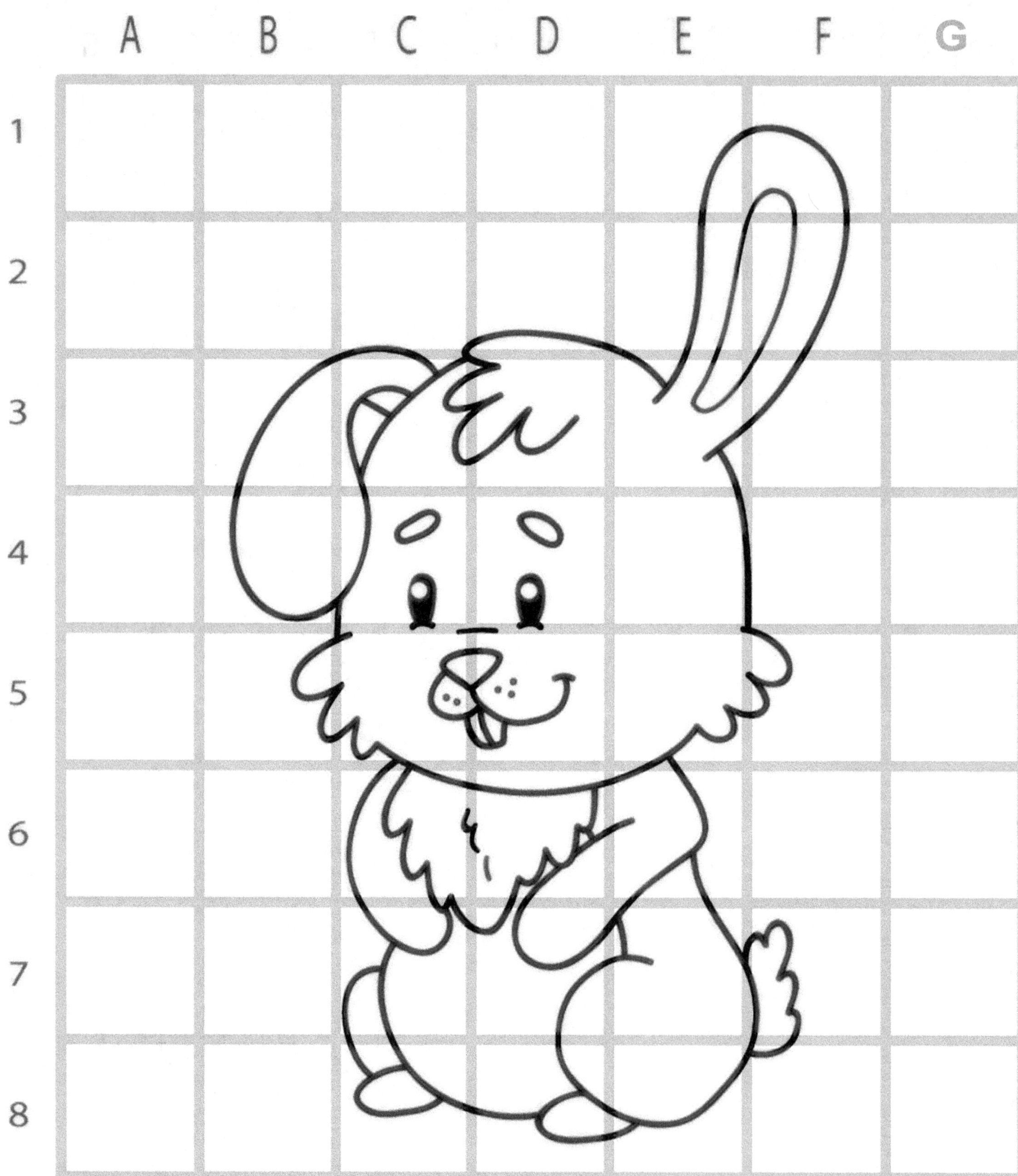

	A	B	C	D	E	F	G
1							
2							
3							
4							
5							
6							
7							
8							

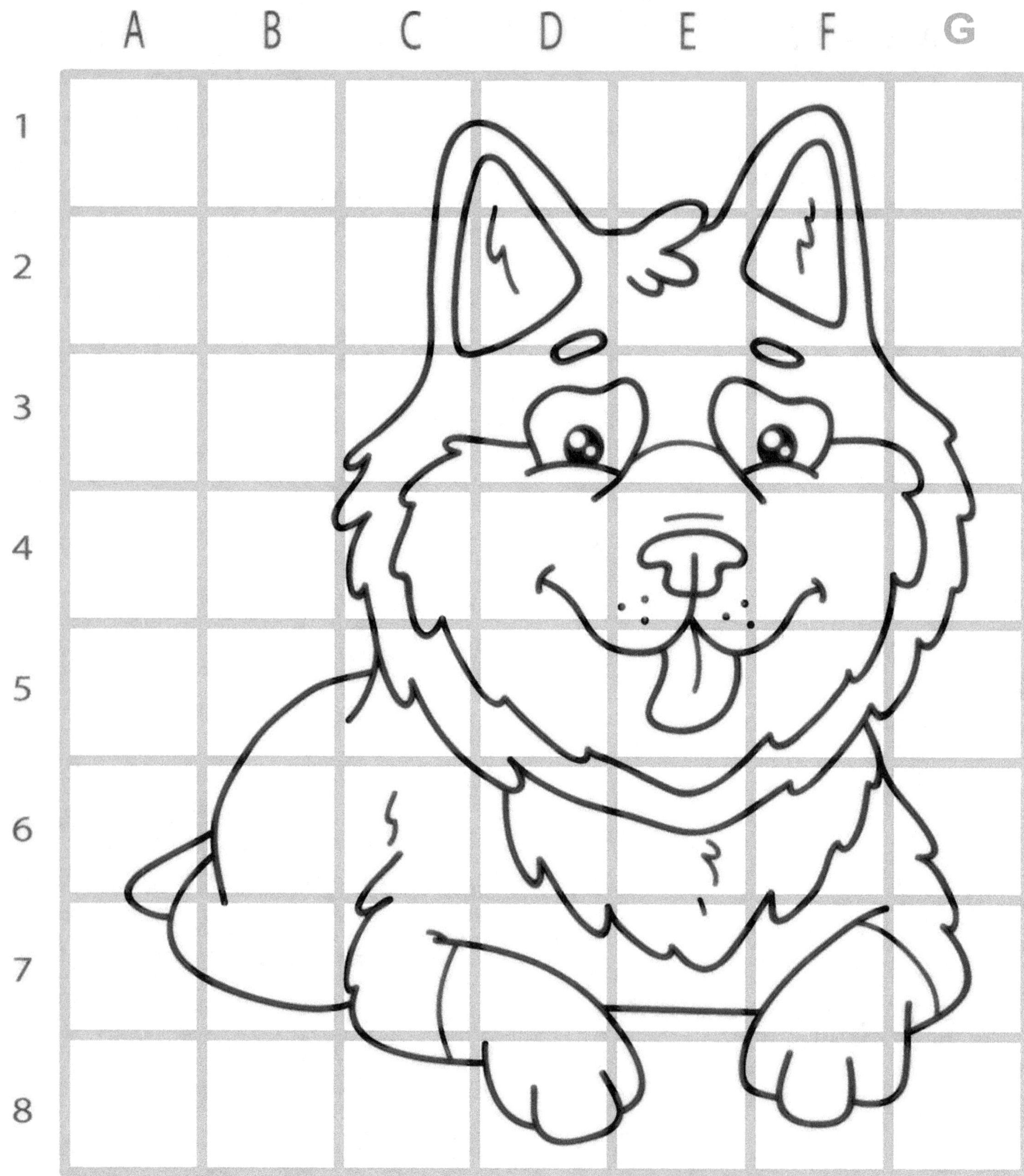

A B C D E F G
1
2
3
4
5
6
7
8

	A	B	C	D	E	F	G
1							
2							
3							
4							
5							
6							
7							
8							

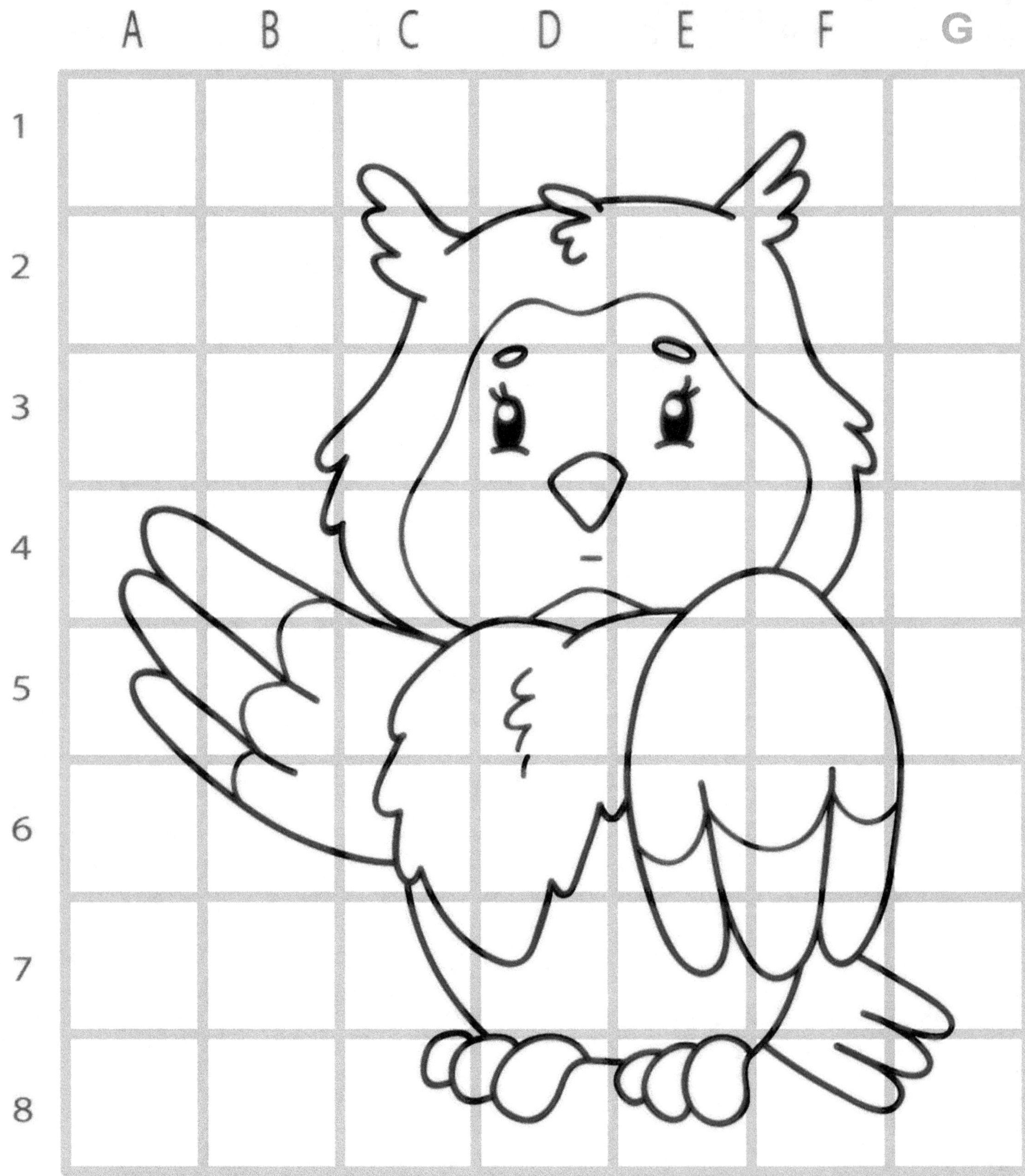

	A	B	C	D	E	F	G
1							
2							
3							
4							
5							
6							
7							
8							

A B C D E F G
1
2
3
4
5
6
7
8

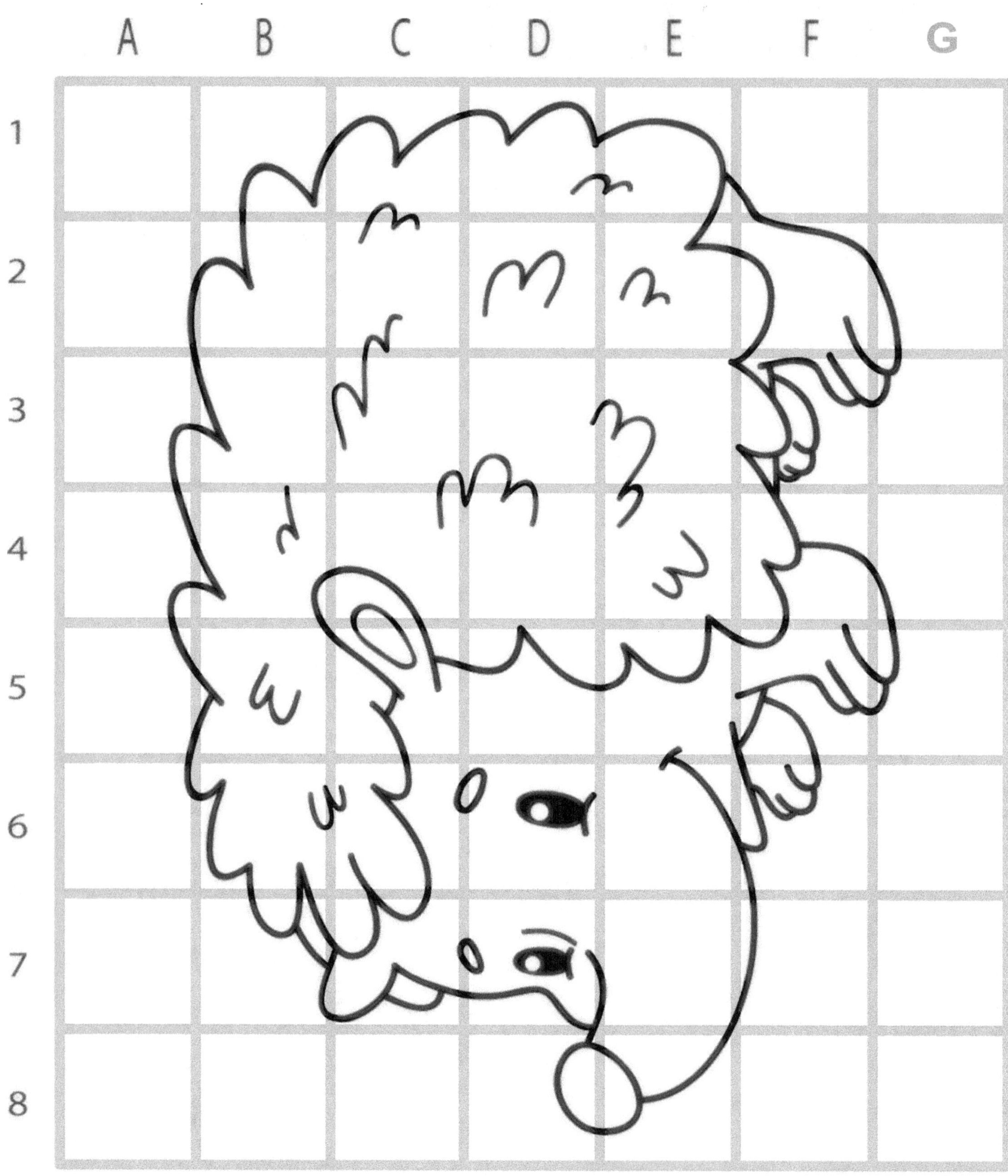

	A	B	C	D	E	F	G
1							
2							
3							
4							
5							
6							
7							
8							

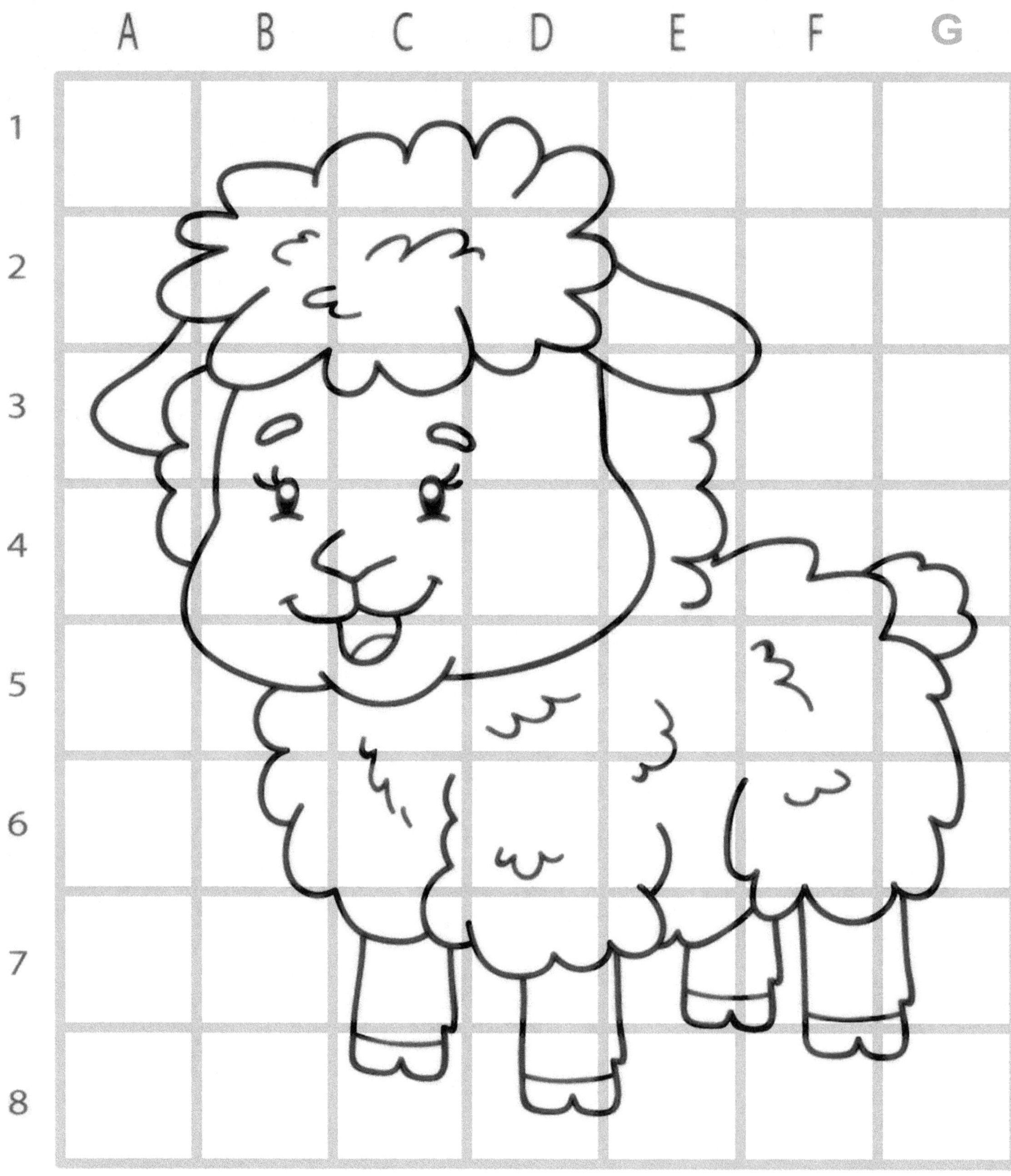

A B C D E F G
1 2 3 4 5 6 7 8

	A	B	C	D	E	F	G
1							
2							
3							
4							
5							
6							
7							
8							

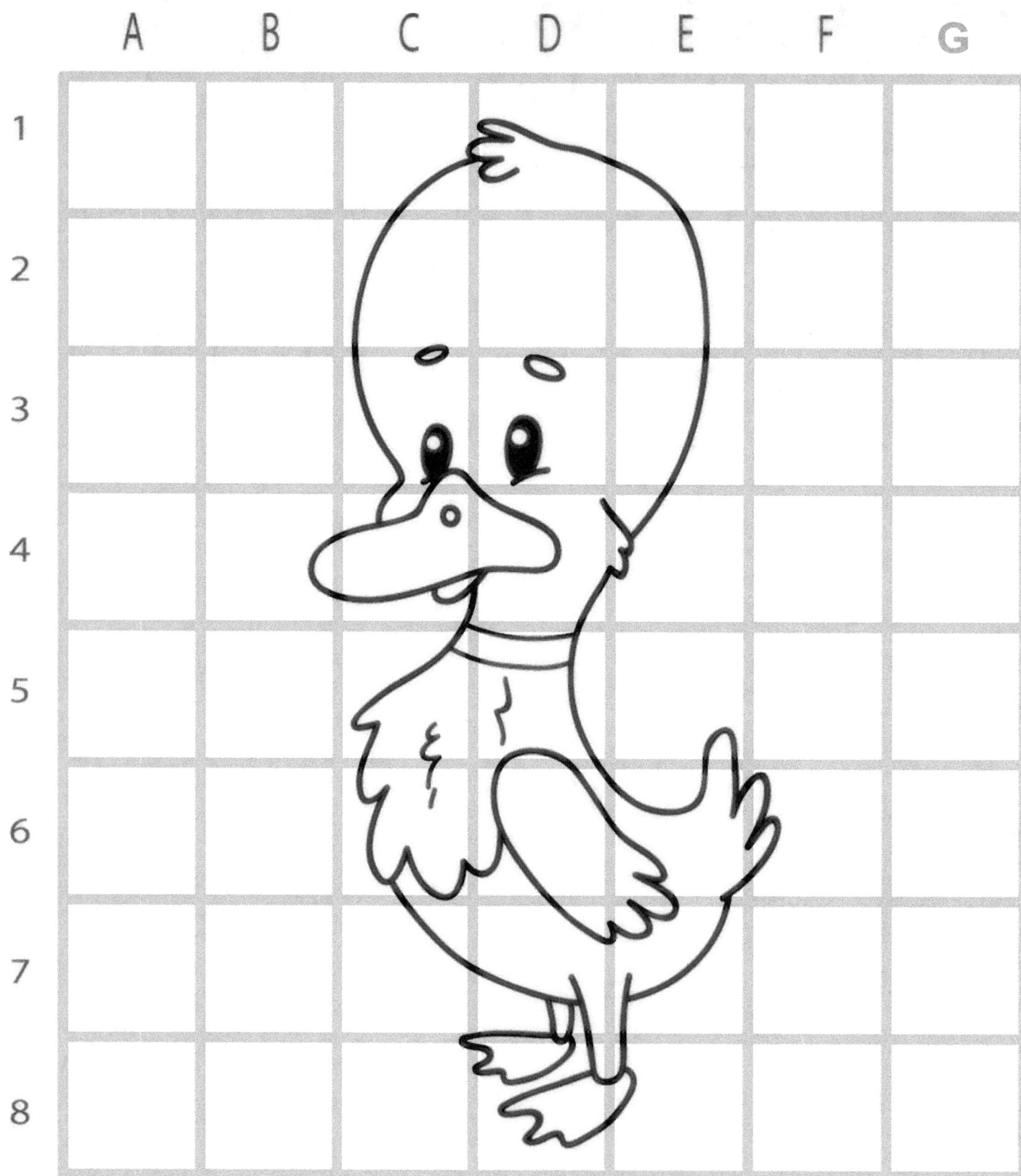

A B C D E F G
1 2 3 4 5 6 7 8

	A	B	C	D	E	F	G
1							
2							
3							
4							
5							
6							
7							
8							

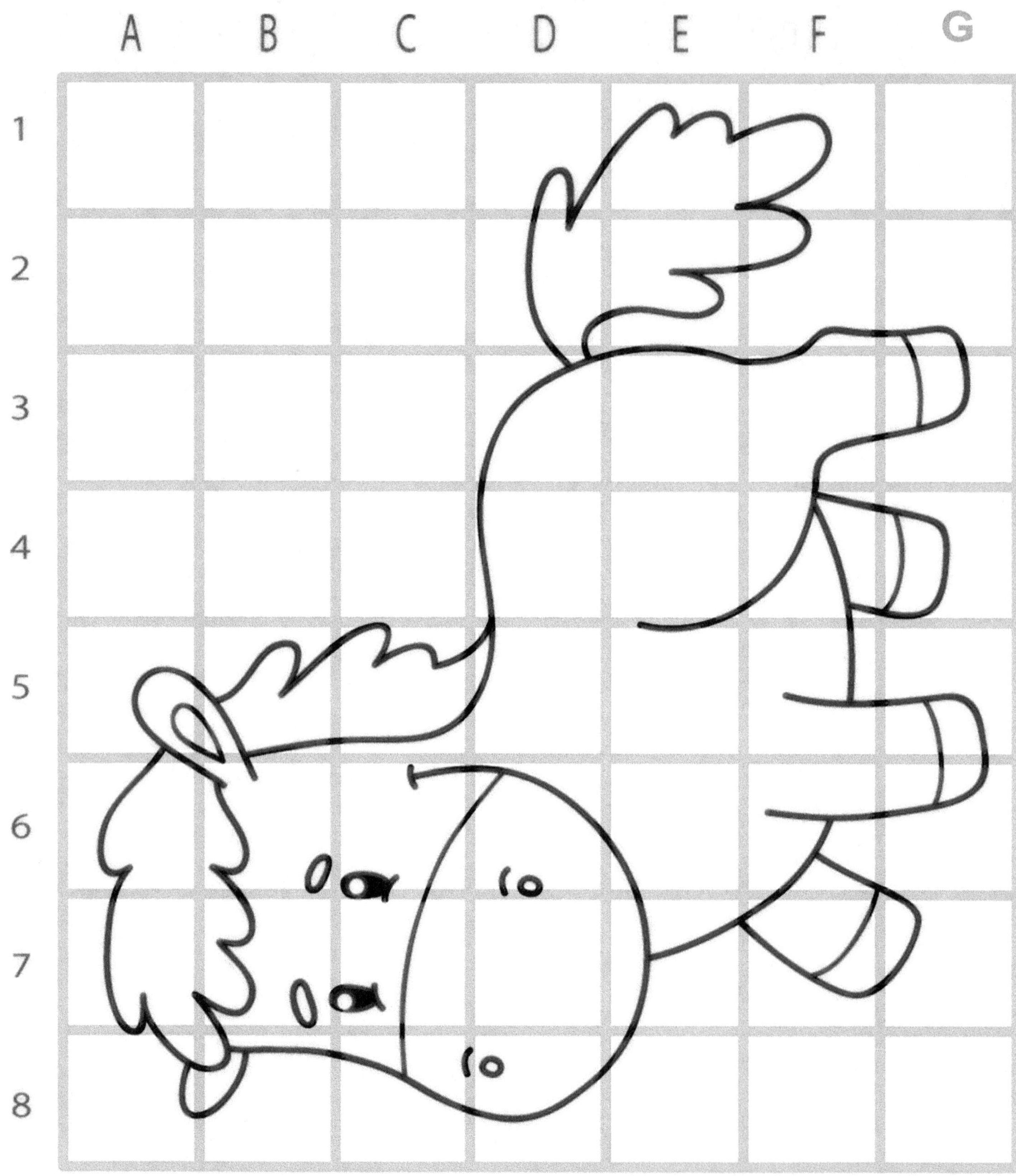

A B C D E F G
1
2
3
4
5
6
7
8

	A	B	C	D	E	F	G
1							
2							
3							
4							
5							
6							
7							
8							

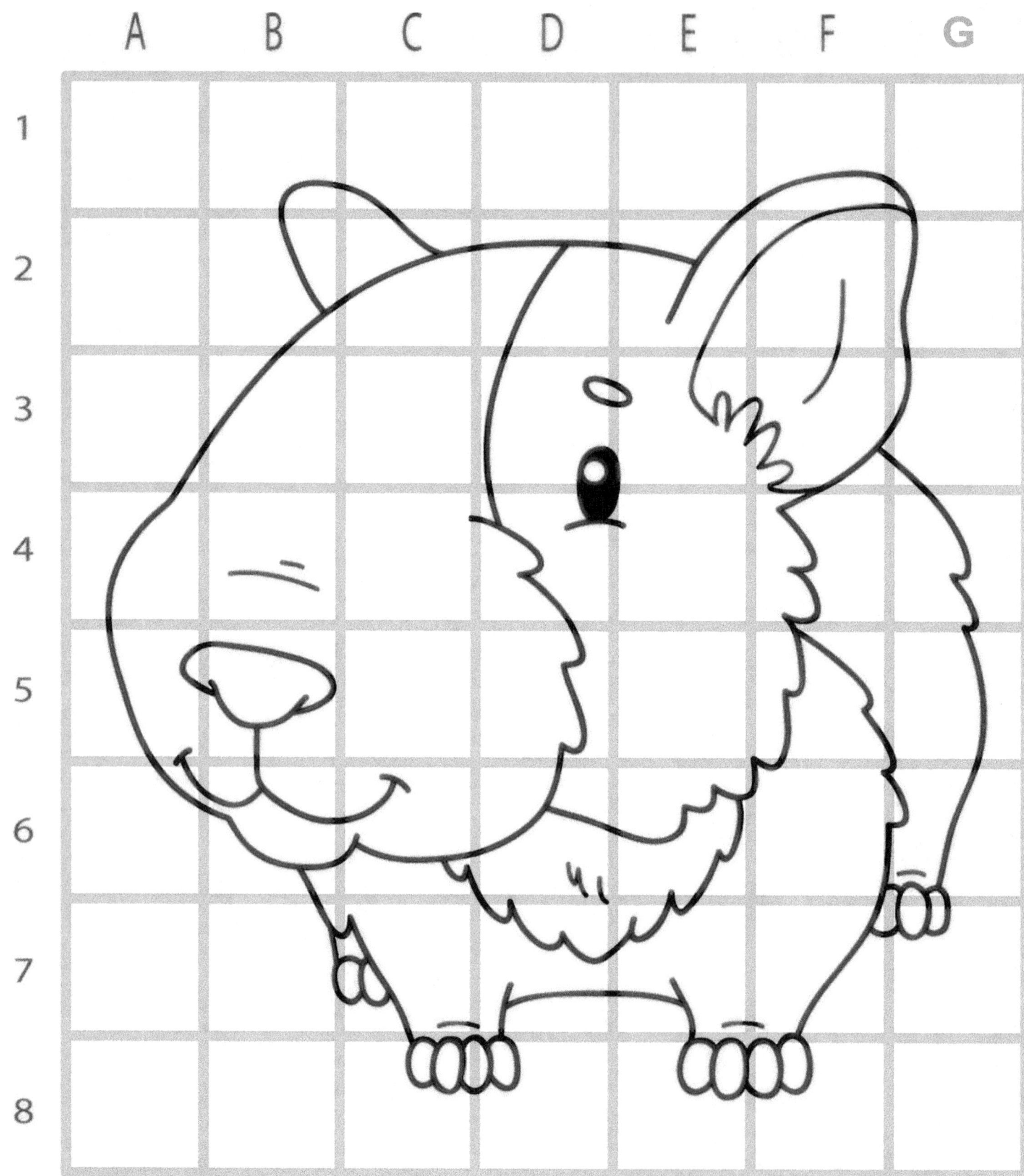

A B C D E F G
1
2
3
4
5
6
7
8

	A	B	C	D	E	F	G
1							
2							
3							
4							
5							
6							
7							
8							

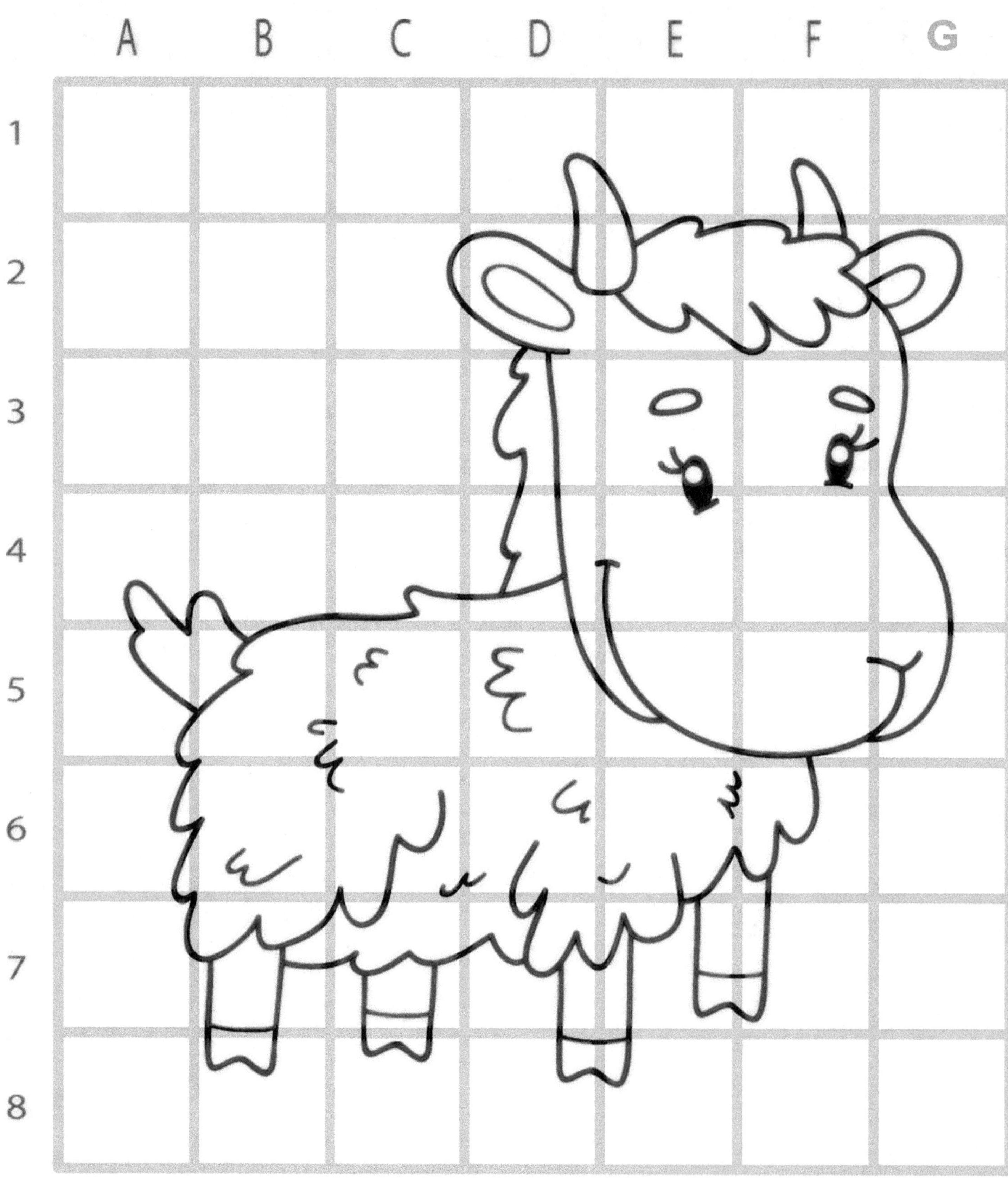

A B C D E F G
1 2 3 4 5 6 7 8

	A	B	C	D	E	F	G
1							
2							
3							
4							
5							
6							
7							
8							

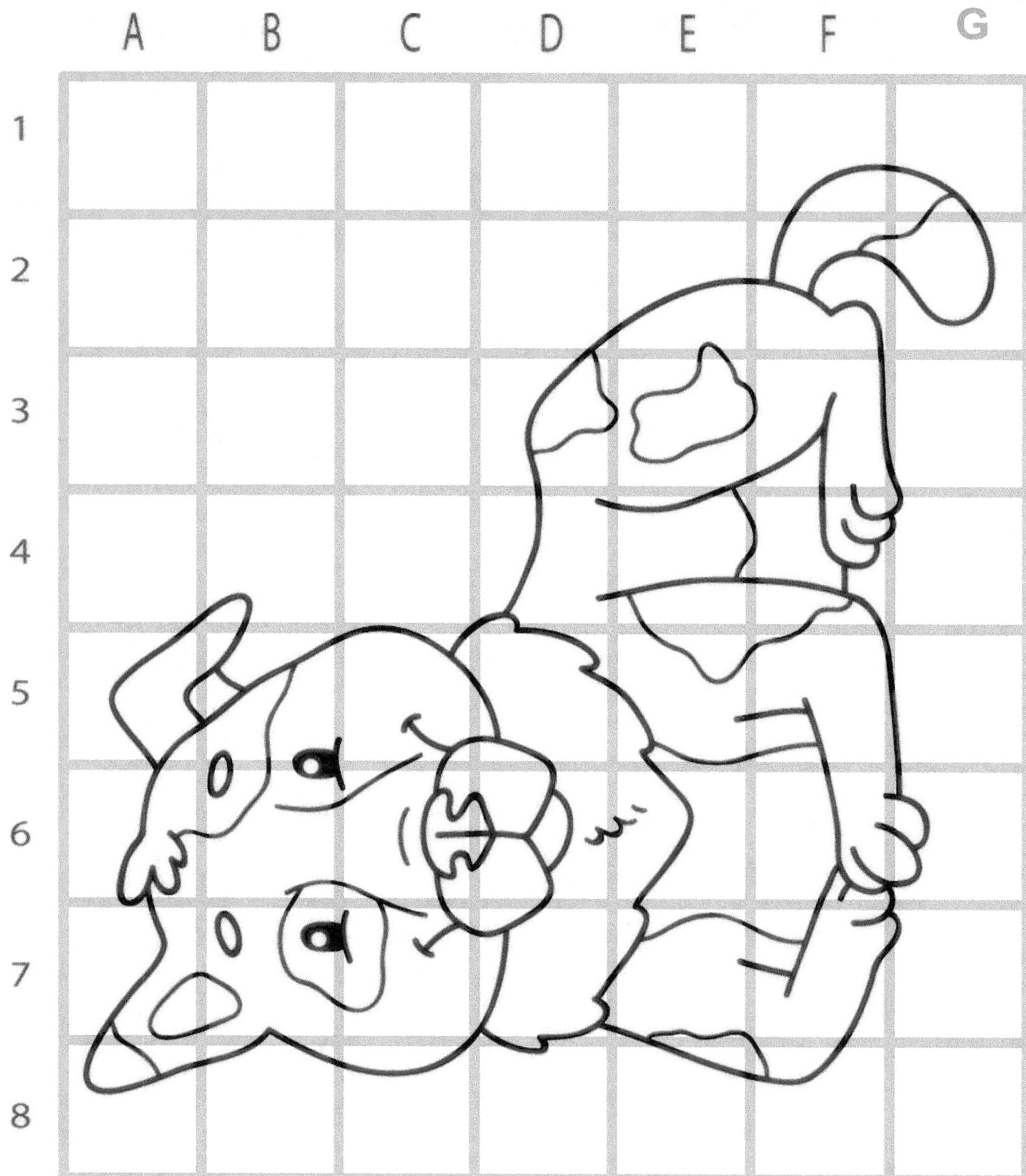

	A	B	C	D	E	F	G
1							
2							
3							
4							
5							
6							
7							
8							

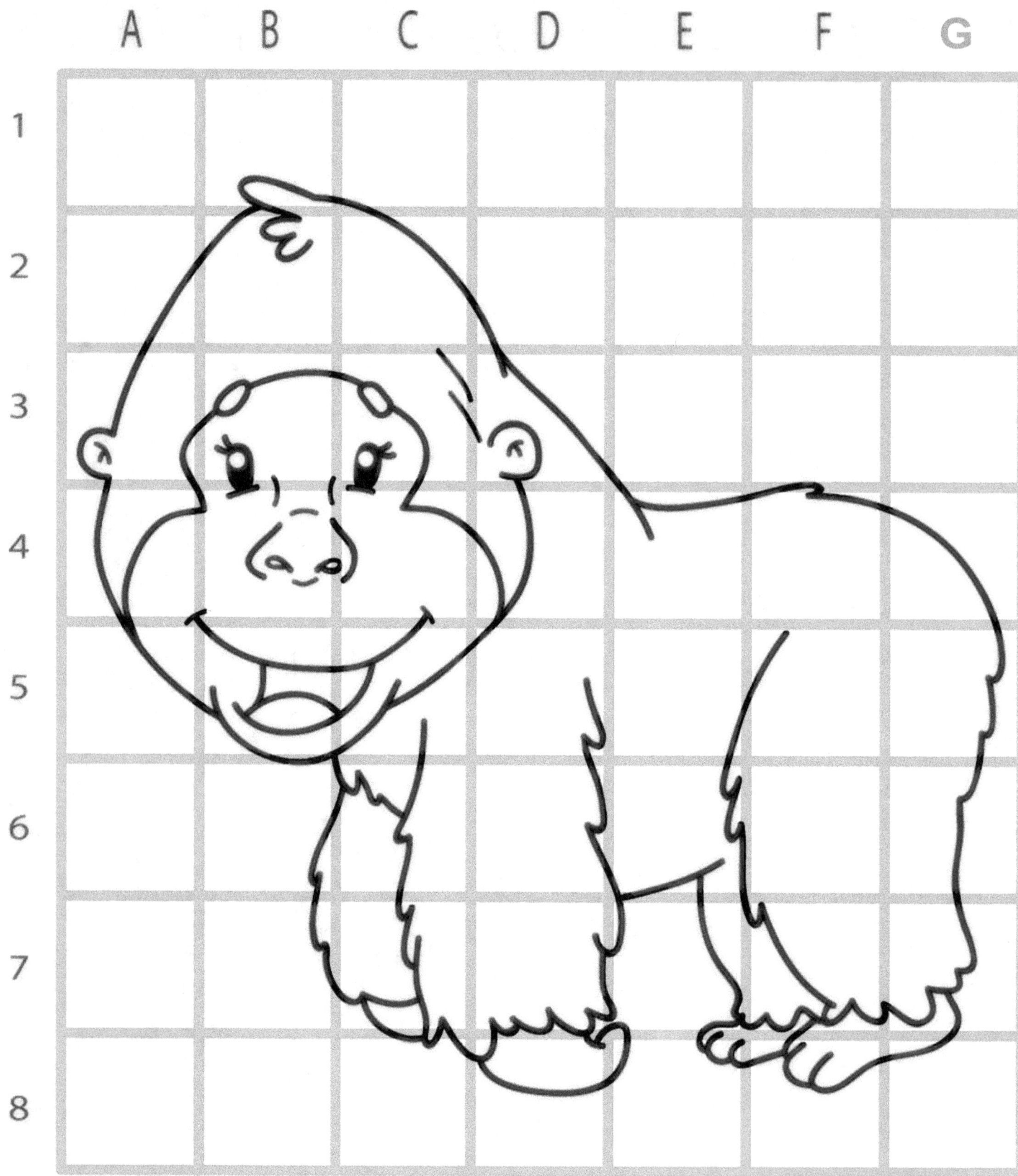

A B C D E F G
1
2
3
4
5
6
7
8

	A	B	C	D	E	F	G
1							
2							
3							
4							
5							
6							
7							
8							

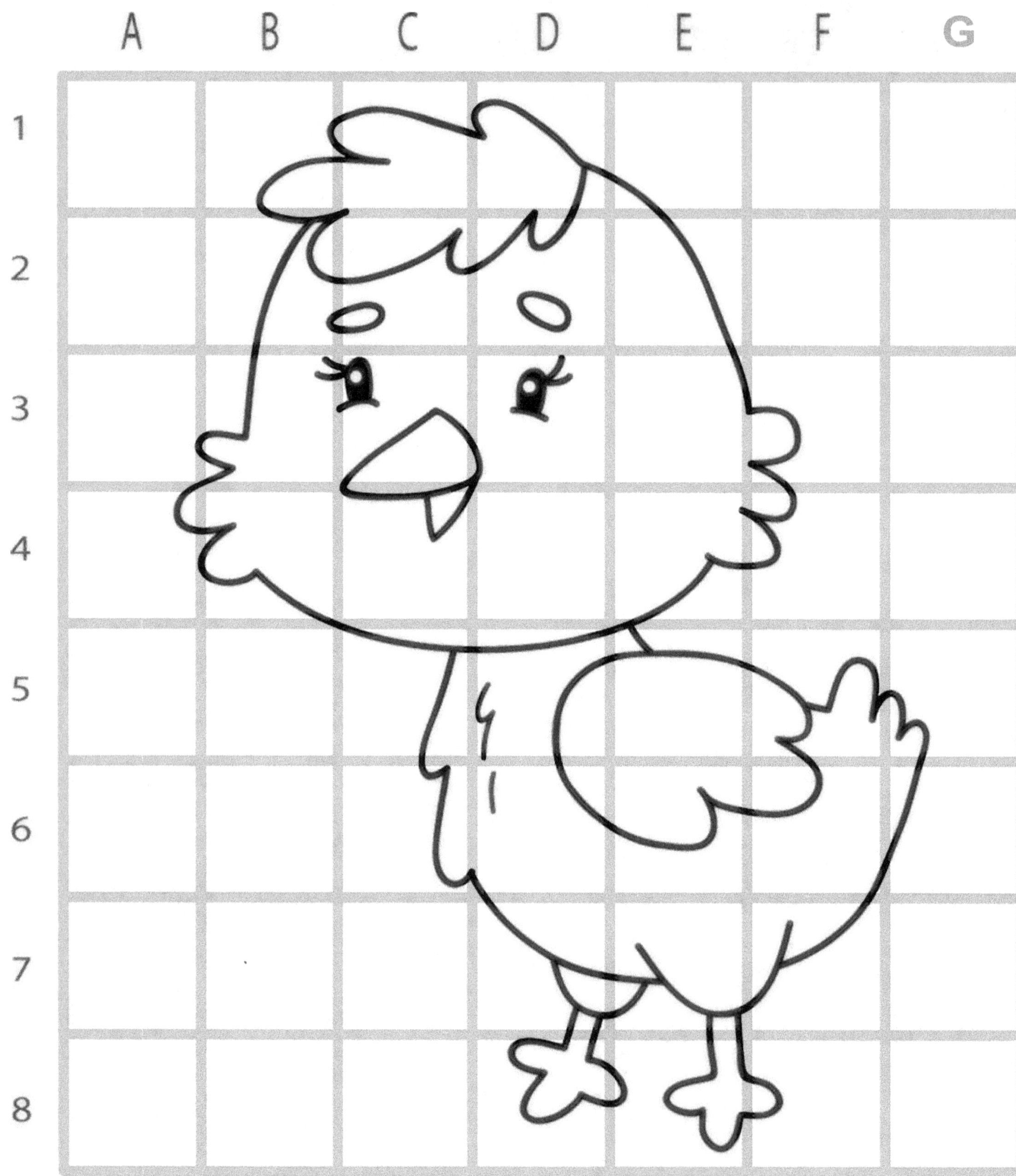

	A	B	C	D	E	F	G
1							
2							
3							
4							
5							
6							
7							
8							

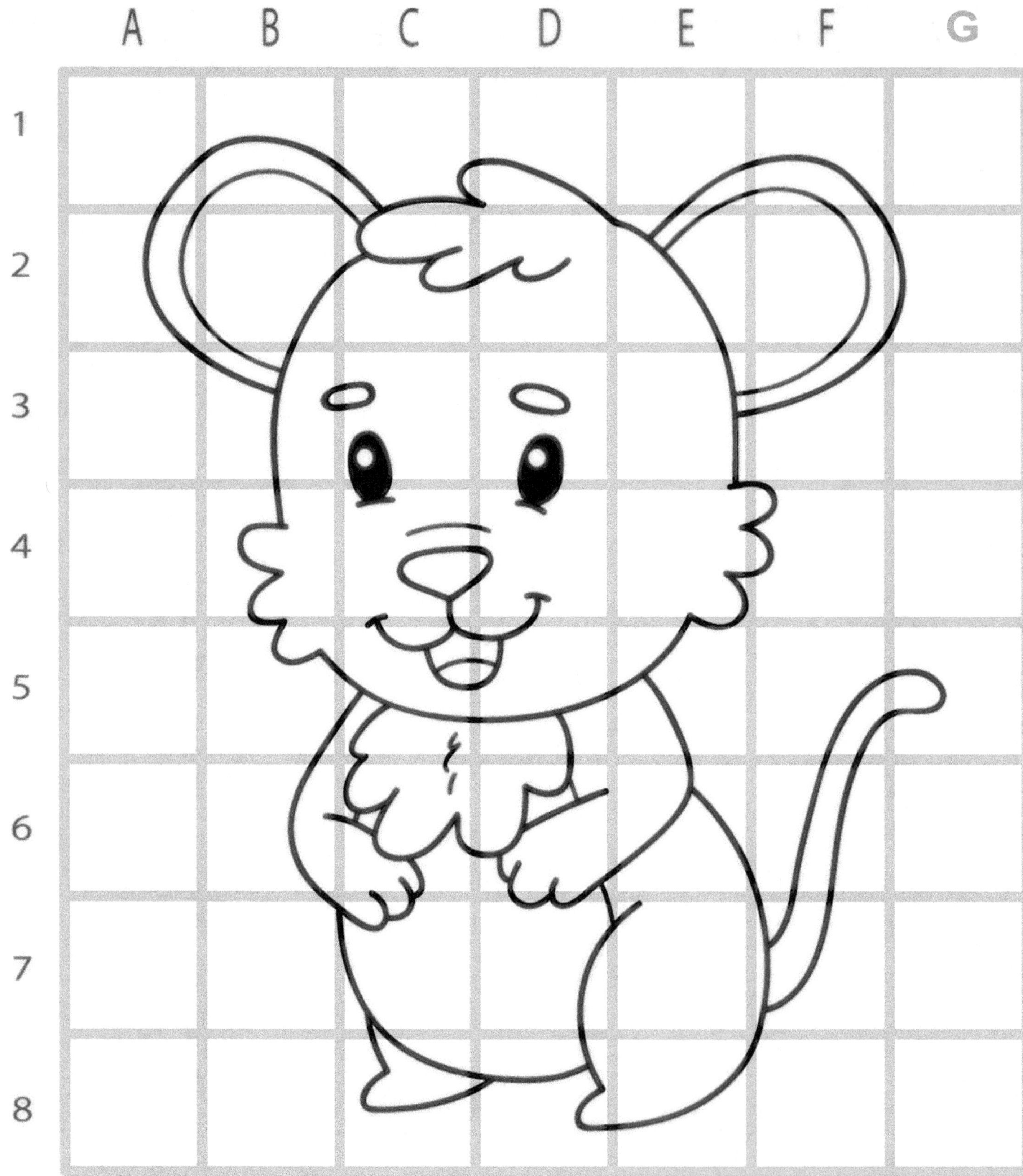

A B C D E F G
1
2
3
4
5
6
7
8

	A	B	C	D	E	F	G
1							
2							
3							
4							
5							
6							
7							
8							

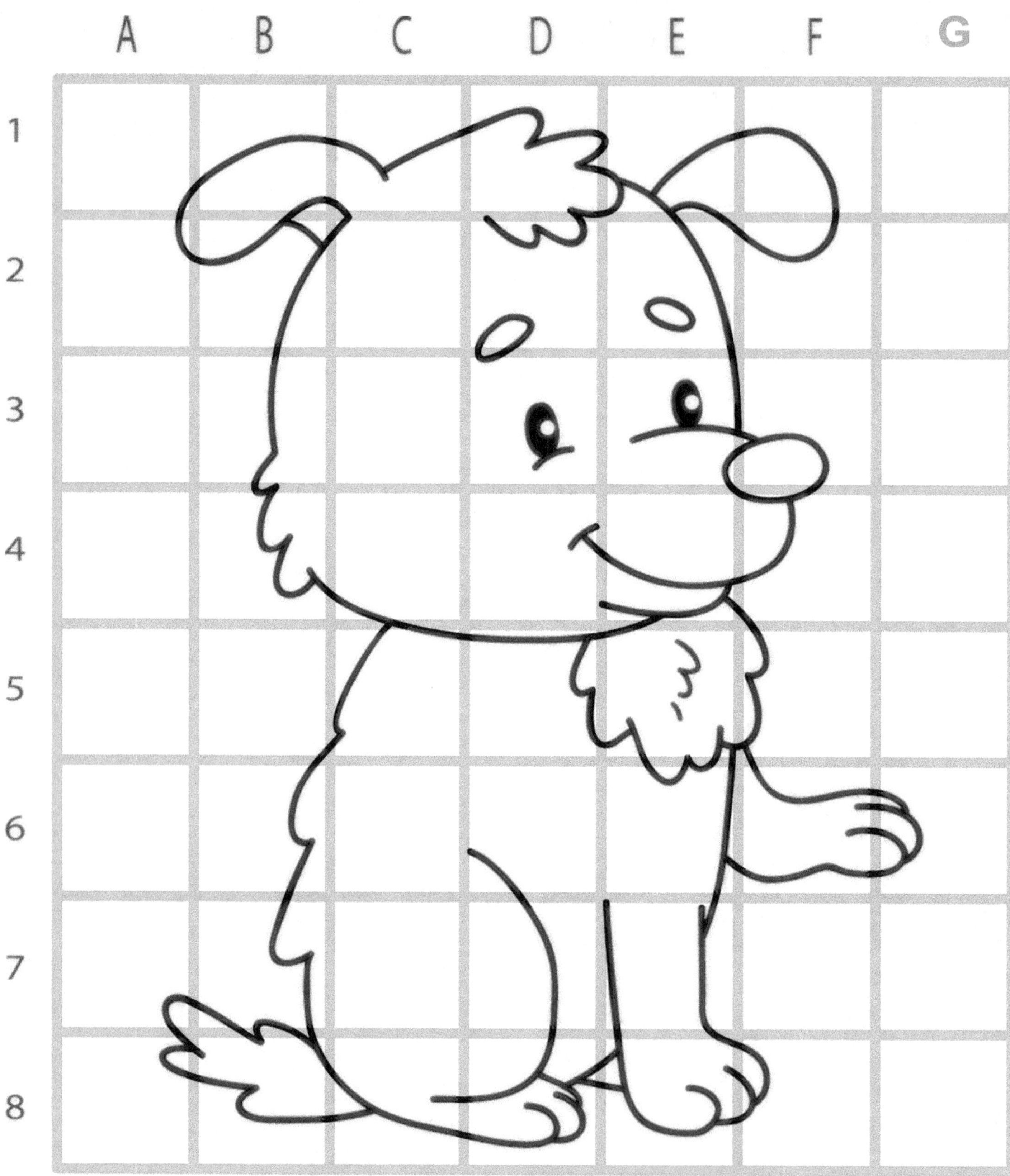

	A	B	C	D	E	F	G
1							
2							
3							
4							
5							
6							
7							
8							

A B C D E F G
1 2 3 4 5 6 7 8

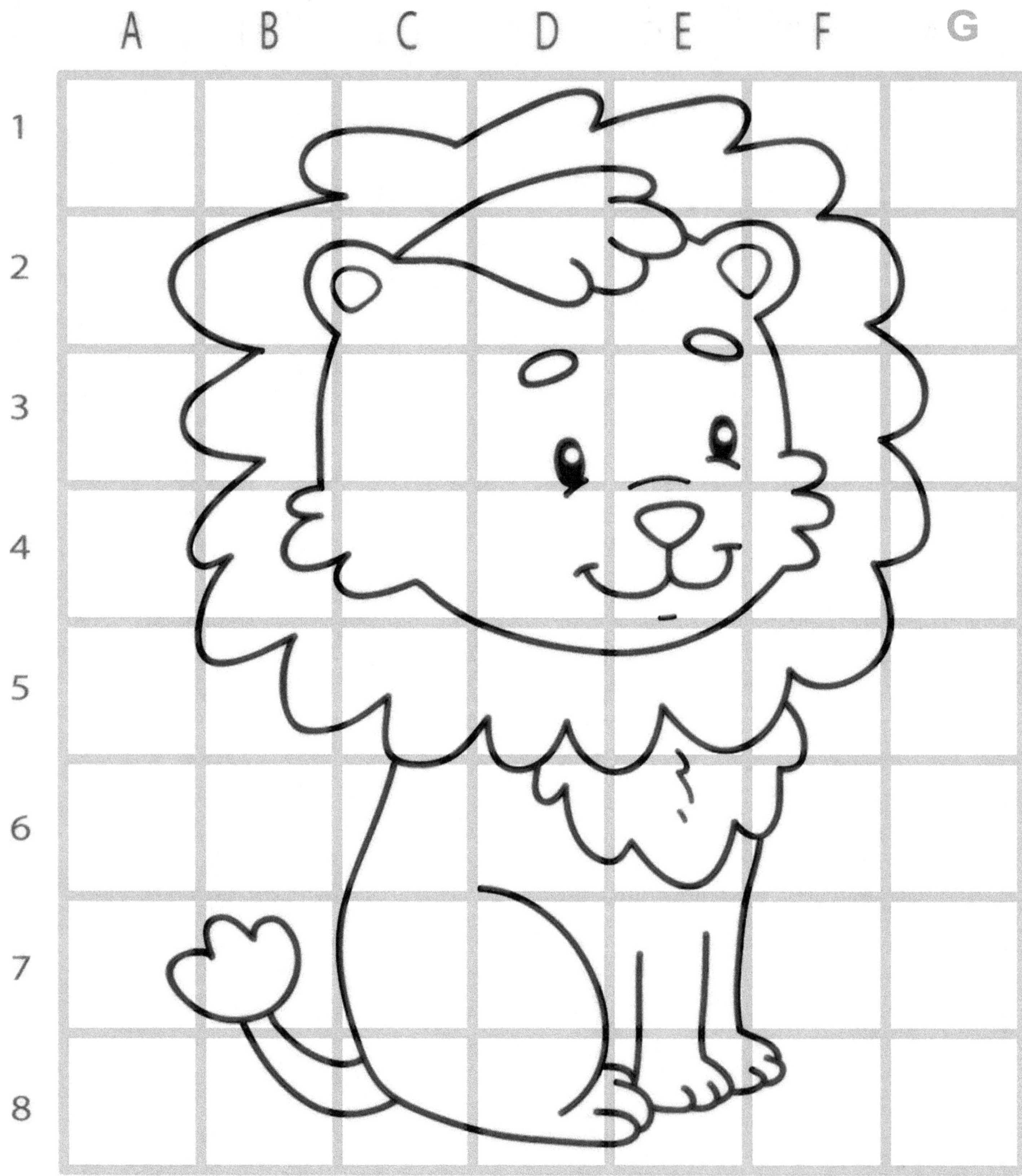

	A	B	C	D	E	F	G
1							
2							
3							
4							
5							
6							
7							
8							

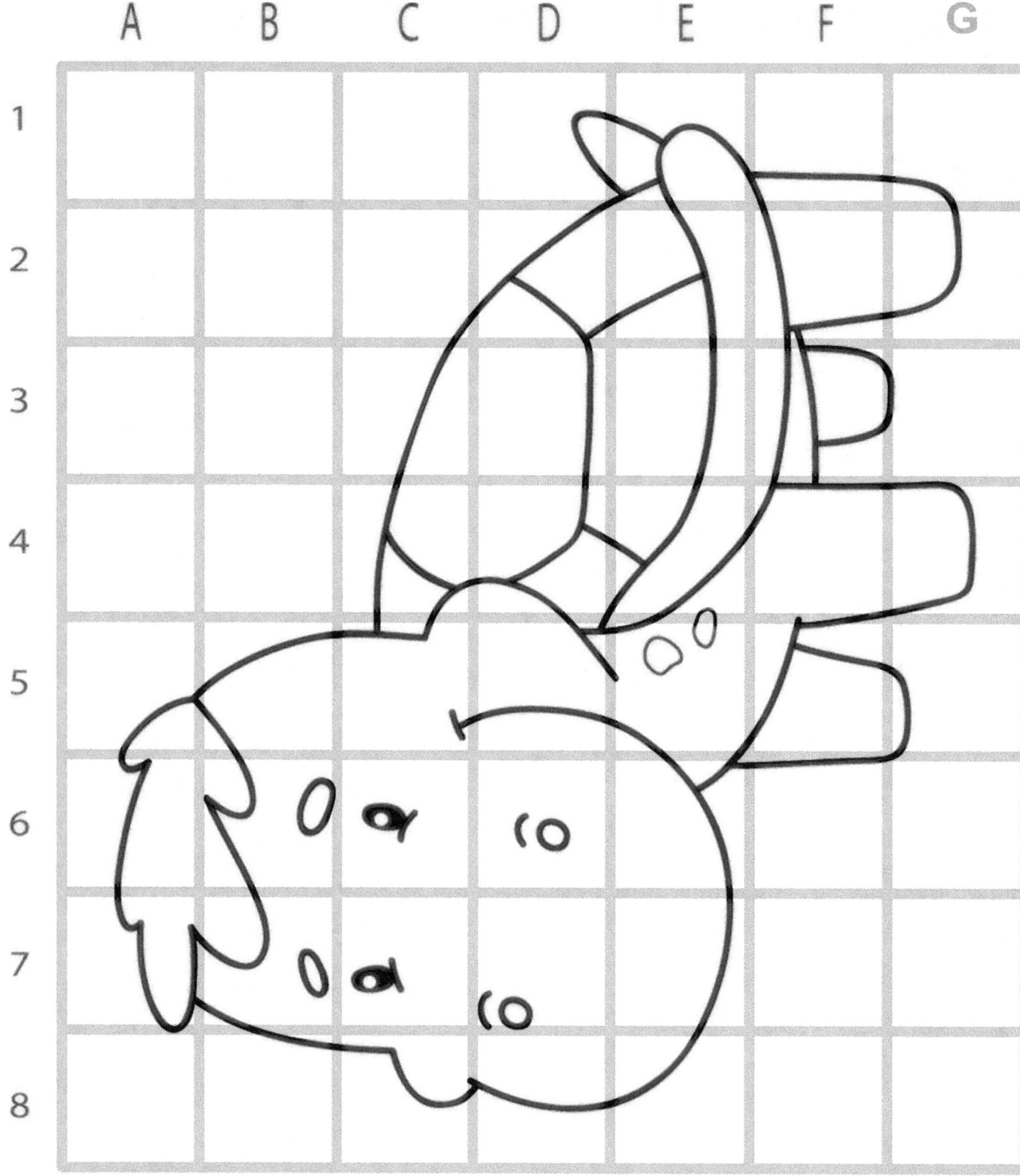

	A	B	C	D	E	F	G
1							
2							
3							
4							
5							
6							
7							
8							

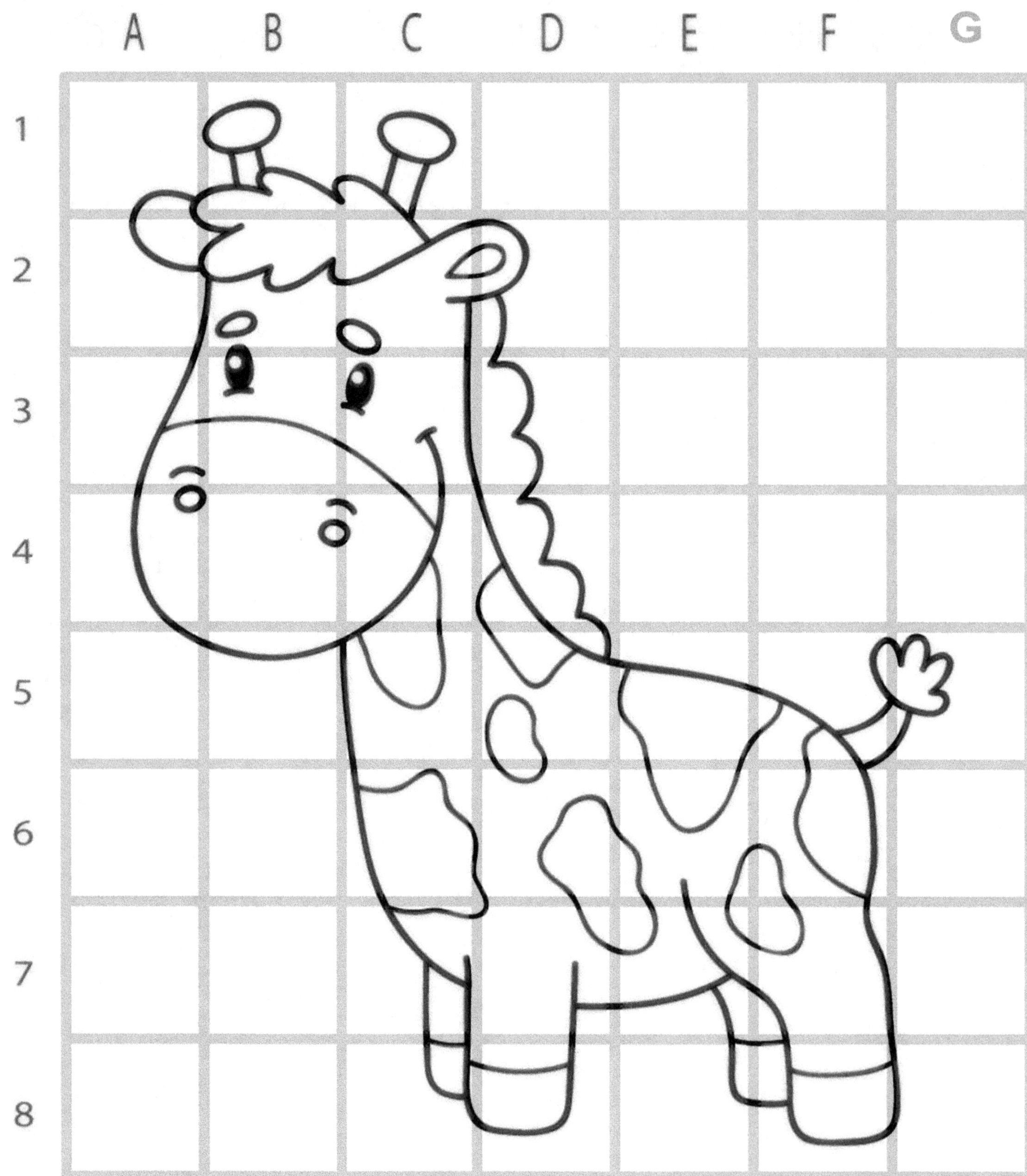

A B C D E F G
1
2
3
4
5
6
7
8

	A	B	C	D	E	F	G
1							
2							
3							
4							
5							
6							
7							
8							

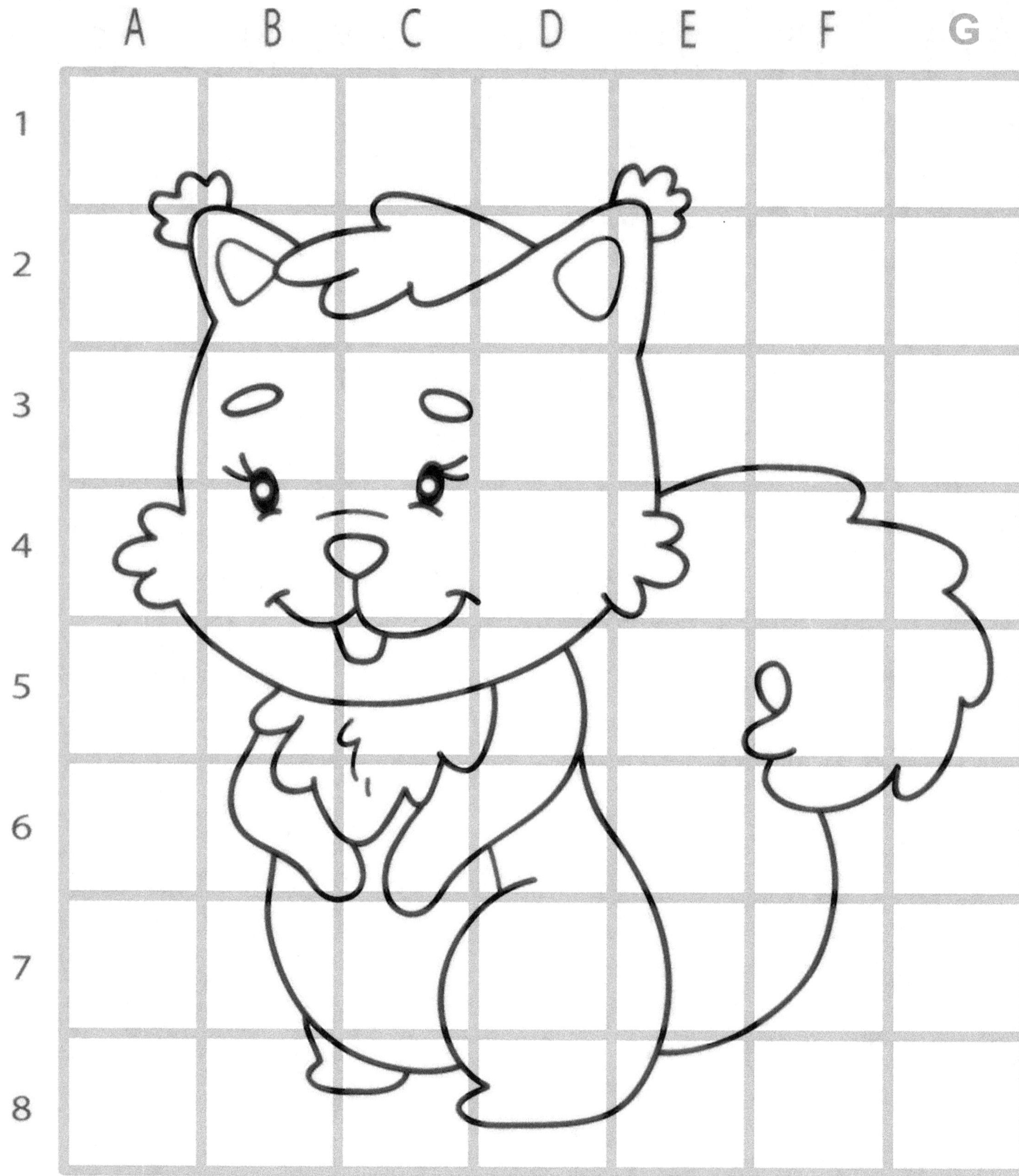

A B C D E F G
1
2
3
4
5
6
7
8

	A	B	C	D	E	F	G
1							
2							
3							
4							
5							
6							
7							
8							

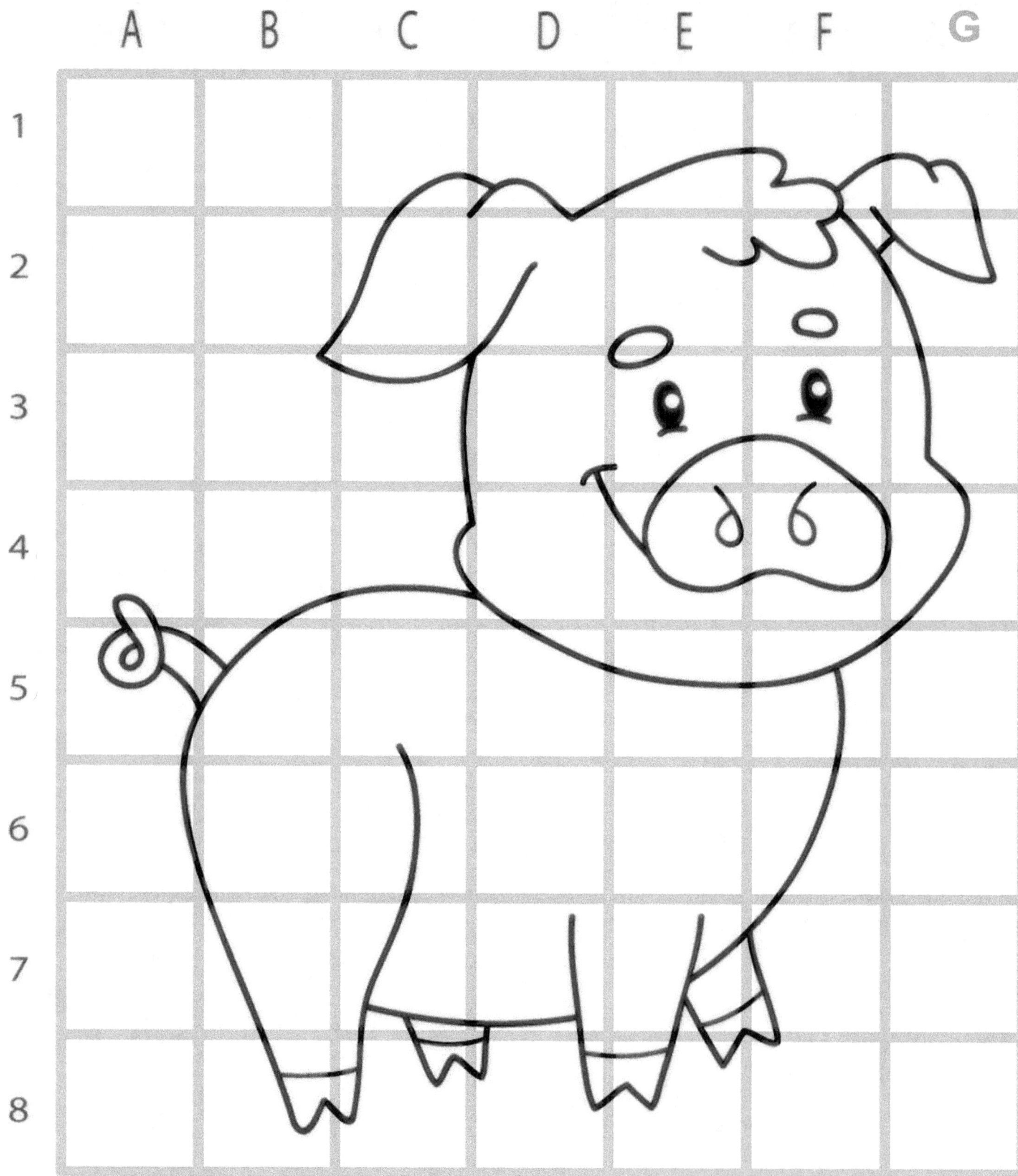
A B C D E F G
1 2 3 4 5 6 7 8

	A	B	C	D	E	F	G
1							
2							
3							
4							
5							
6							
7							
8							

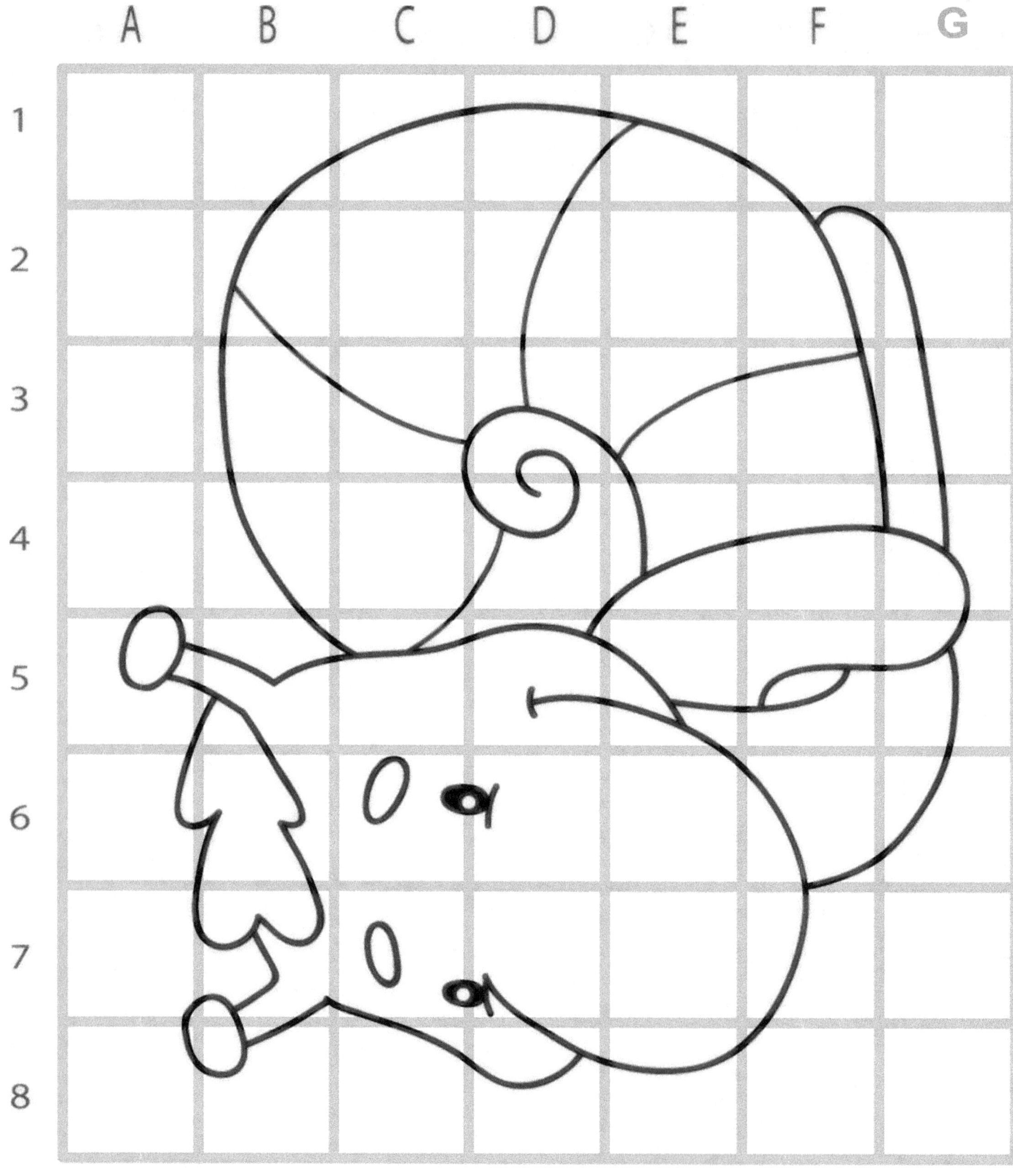

	A	B	C	D	E	F	G
1							
2							
3							
4							
5							
6							
7							
8							

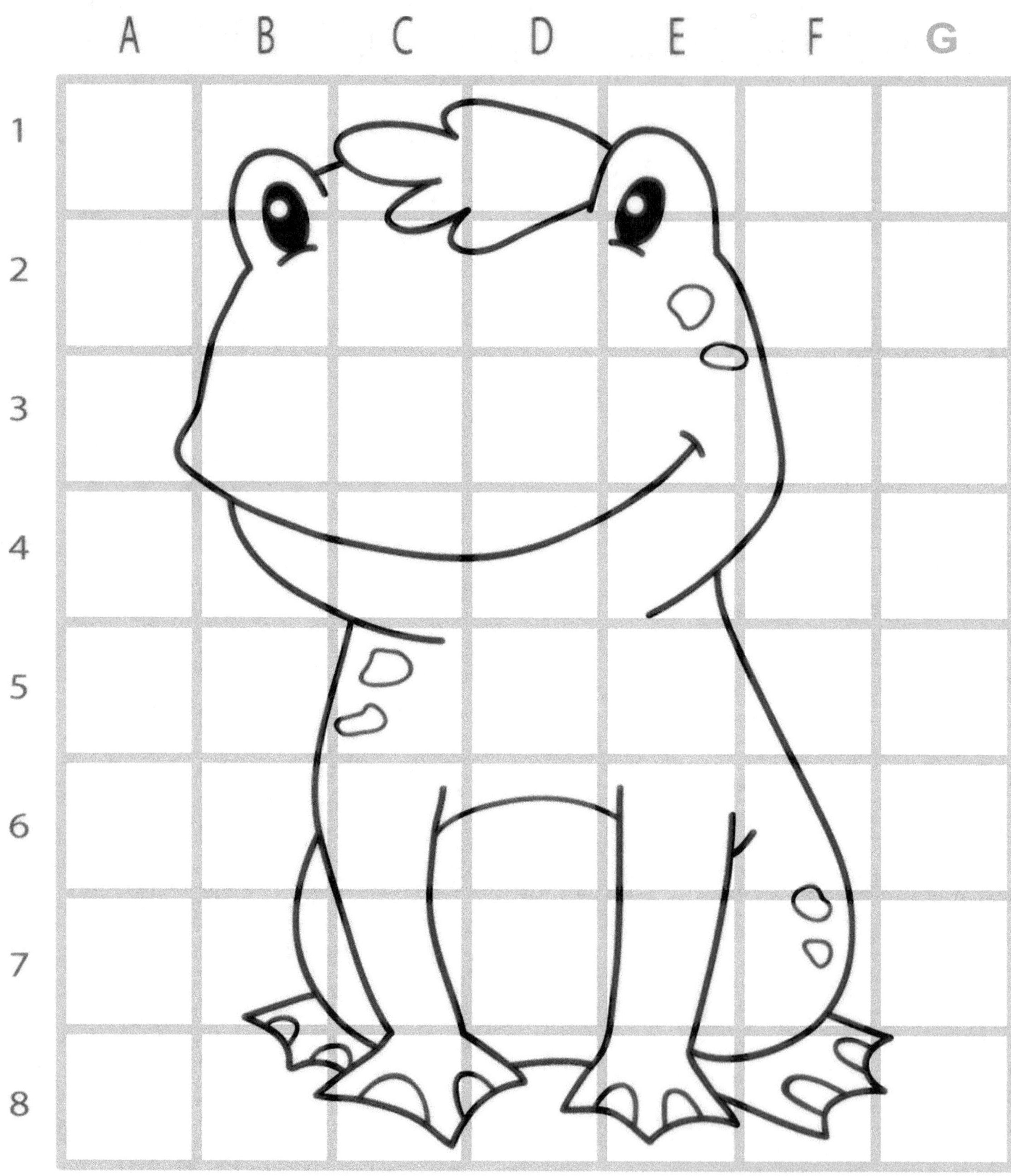

A B C D E F G
1
2
3
4
5
6
7
8

	A	B	C	D	E	F	G
1							
2							
3							
4							
5							
6							
7							
8							

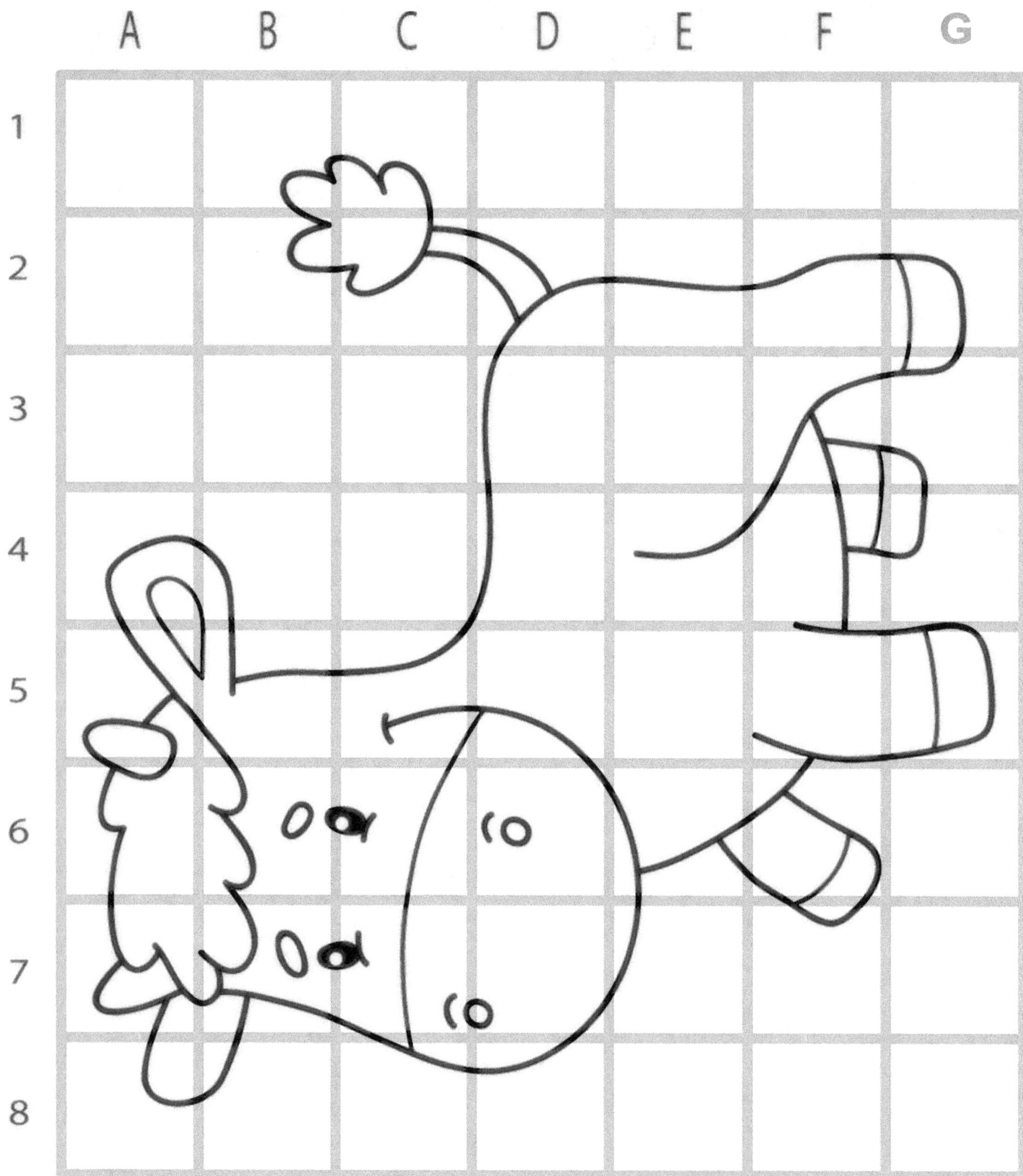

	A	B	C	D	E	F	G
1							
2							
3							
4							
5							
6							
7							
8							

9 781949 651041